The Mountains of America

The Mountains of America

From Alaska to the Great Smokies

Text by Franklin Russell
Introduction by Edward Abbey

Text by Franklin Russell
Harry N. Abrams, Inc., Publishers, New York

Library of Congress Cataloging in Publication Data
Main entry under title:
The Mountains of America.
1. Mountains—North America—Pictorial works.
I. Russell, Franklin, II. Rugoff, Milton
III. Rayfield, Susan
GB521.M68   551.4'3'0973   75-9972
ISBN 0-8109-0360-1

Published by Harry N. Abrams, Incorporated, New York, 1975

Prepared and produced by Chanticleer Press, Inc.
Color reproductions by Fontana and Bonomi, Milan, Italy
Printed and bound by Amilcare Pizzi, S.p.A., Milan, Italy

Design: Massimo Vignelli

Title Page: An autumn dawn on Mount Rainier. *(Harald Sund)*

Contents

Introduction by Edward Abbey

What am I doing here? I am no expert on mountains. I am not a
geographer, understand little of geology. I have never gone near the
foothills of Annapurna. I am certainly no true mountaineer or climber.
My notion of a mountain climb is a hike up the trail to Mount Whitney or
a scramble up one of Colorado's easier 14,000-footers. My qualifications
for writing the introduction to this book lie in a certain reluctant but
lasting affection I have for these wrinkles, bulges, eruptions, and
fractures on the earth's surface which we call mountains.

For me the fascination began in the Allegheny Mountains of western
Pennsylvania, on the little submarginal farm where I was born and
raised. Though called "mountains" on the map, those ancient and rolling
hills are but the northern fringe of the real Appalachians, which are in
turn only remnants of a much greater range that once existed there.
Nevertheless, the Alleghenies are high enough to excite the imagination
of a boy. My latent acrophilia was brought out early by excursions upward
through the pastures under the lightning-blasted shagbark hickories—
trees thus endowed with magical powers, according to Shawnee Indian
lore—up through the cornfields where we labored (not too hard) in the
stifling heat of September, up through the second-growth woods of maple,
white oak, beech, poplar, and walnut, up the path to the little spring
where we kept a pint Mason jar up-ended on a root, and beyond the
spring to the summit of the hill, where tracts of wood shared living space
with the wide open fields of hay.

Where does the line "High on a windy hill" come from? Some popular song?
Anyway, it evokes at once the spirit and the atmosphere of those skyward
excursions. Clouds soaring by, the soft and melting clouds of Pennsylvania
on the gentle Watteau blue of the Pennsylvania sky. Down below—far
below I would have said then—I could see the red barns, the white
farmhouses, the green and yellow fields, meanders of sulfurous Crooked
Creek, the winding ways of the country roads passing among the hills
from farm to farm, narrow lanes surfaced with red slag from the mines;
we called them "red dog" roads.

From the hills of home to the heights of the Himalayas is a long journey.
All downward, maybe. A journey which, in any case, I have yet to finish.
But the first step was westward to the Rockies. Seventeen years old and
ignorant as any other yokel, I took off one summer to see the country,
thinking it might be my last chance. According to the newspapers of
that year (1944), I and a million other adolescents were scheduled to land
on the mainland of Japan the following year for reasons obscure to me
then but like other things taken for granted. What I wanted to see, far
more than the shores of Honshu Island, were the Rocky Mountains.

For two weeks I hitchhiked west, working my way through the Mid-
west and the wheatfields of South Dakota, gathering winter wheat
in its heavy, dew-soaked sheaves. Paid off, I traveled farther
west and on one bright sunny day in middle June, walking out past the
junkyards, feedlots, and gas stations of a small town in Wyoming, I saw
for the first time in my life the shining ramparts of the Rocky Mountains.
The snow-covered range gleamed in the morning sun, sixty or seventy
miles away, floating like a shoal of clouds across the western horizon. To
me, who had never before seen hills higher than three or four thousand
feet above sea level, it was a fantastic sight. A dream. The magic and
magnetic mountains. Love at first sight.

After that came many others, a lifetime of mountains viewed in the
summer of youth. I saw the Wind River Range, the Sawtooth Mountains,
the Absarokas, and the Bitterroots. On to the Pacific and a glimpse of the
Cascades, the coastal ranges, and then down to California, where I spent
a month wandering through the High Sierra from Yosemite to Mount
Whitney and down the other side to Lone Pine in the Owens Valley.
Hitchhiking across the Mojave Desert in August I had my first view and
taste of desert mountains: the Calicoes, the Chocolates, the Panamints,
the Chuckawallas and the Needle Peaks of Arizona at the Colorado River.
Out of the infernal valley, I rode the rails back into high country again
and saw Music Mountain, Bill Williams Mountain, the San Francisco
Peaks near Flagstaff, and on to the mountains of New Mexico—Mount
Taylor, El Ladron, the Sandias, the Manzanos and the Sangre de Cristos.
By that time my summer was over. Then, home to Pennsylvania.

Only a view, a taste of mountains: I could not say I had come to know

6

them in any significant way. All that I had learned really was something about myself. I had discovered that I was the kind of person who cannot live comfortably, tolerably, on all-flat terrain. For the sake of inner equilibrium, there has to be at least one mountain range on at least one of the four quarters of the horizon—and not more than a day's walk away. Shipped to Italy in 1945 by the United States Army, the first thing I did on my first weekend pass was trudge up the cinder slopes of Mount Vesuvius for a look into its evil, stinking crater. I had missed the latest eruption of Vesuvius by one year, but there was enough thermal activity still going on down in there, in the volcano's burbling pit, to give me an idea of the real nature of this strange and ambiguous planet we live on. Thoreau wished to be appointed Inspector of Snowstorms. I wanted there and then to be an Inspector of Volcanoes. Big ones only. Months later, in the middle of winter, I made a railway tour of the Swiss Alps. The spectacle of the Matterhorn from Zermatt, the sight of the Jungfrau from Interlaken, roused ancestral memories: my father's father came from a village in Canton Bern. One might as well give up and become, I thought, like Herr Settembrini in *The Magic Mountain*, a philosopher of high places. I would never again want to live away from them.

It's all very well to look at mountains, I tell myself, and very nice to have a view of snow-covered peaks out the picture window. But why should anyone want to climb them? A proper question, as fitting now as when it was asked of George H. Leigh-Mallory back in the early twenties. Why? is always a good question, the one question that distinguishes the human from all of the other brutes. Mallory's answer, "Because it's there," is not entirely satisfactory, except of course to other climbers, who climb first and make up answers afterward. To the question, Why? Mallory answers in effect, Why not? and disappears forever into Mount Everest's wind and snow at 28,000 feet, evading the question. His answer is at once too broad and too narrow—all embracing and yet not adequate. The nonclimber demands a fuller reply. *And it would have been forthcoming.* In my opinion Mallory and his fellow climber Andrew Irvine did actually make it to the summit of Everest on that desperate day in early June, 1924. When last seen they had surmounted all serious obstacles except the weather and the lateness of the day; they were less than a thousand feet from the top. This was Mallory's third serious attempt and he probably felt, as Thoreau had said, "now or never." Never mind that they were five hours behind schedule; no matter that they'd have to descend in darkness. This was the best opportunity for the mountaineer's ultimate victory they would ever know. "Why not?" thought Mallory, plodding on and upward. And "What the hell," said Irvine. And they went on, and made it, too; they stood for a few moments on the top of the world, and planted the expedition flag there as sign of their conquest. But of course the two climbers never found their way back down, and so we do not have Mallory's answer to the question. We have only two more martyrs for the hagiography of mountain climbing and the single ice ax, known to have been Mallory's, made by Willish of Tasch, which British climbers found on the northeast ridge of Everest in 1933—nine years after the Assumption of Mallory and Irvine.

Why? Why climb them? It is not merely death by falling which threatens the climber. Such accidents can generally be avoided through care, skill, patience, the proper equipment. More difficult is the misery and sickness of mountaineering, especially above 20,000 feet. In that realm of everlasting ice and snow, where I for one have no intention (probably) of ever setting foot, the human body encounters varieties of stress unknown to lowlanders. Nausea, loss of appetite, cruel headaches, heart strain, pulmonary edema, and pulmonary embolism can afflict even the young and healthy, compounding such routine hazards of high altitudes as frostbite, hypothermia, and pneumonia. At least fourteen men are known to have died in the various assaults, so far, upon Everest. Not so long ago eight Russian climbers died of exhaustion and exposure at 22,000 feet in the Pamirs. In the first successful climb of Annapurna by Maurice Herzog several of his climbers lost fingers and toes because of frostbite. In Hillary's 1961 Himalayan expedition all of his men suffered severely from altitude sickness after months spent above 19,000 feet; one member of the party had to have both feet amputated.

Those are the major difficulties but we have not yet mentioned simple exhaustion, the painful ordeal of dragging one foot after another, against all reason and gravity, up over rock and snow toward the sky, with pack on back, in the drudgery of unnatural effort which begins at the very foot of the mountain. Here I can speak from personal experience. I find that first step upward always so difficult that each time I begin the ascent of a mountain I swear to myself, "Never again." I say, and mean it, "This is the last time." There is something about an uphill hike that always seems so *unnecessary*. The body objects, the heart and lungs complain, and gravity, with arms of lead, drags at every limb to pull down our pride and vanity. And yet the weariness of it all is soon forgotten and a month or a year later we're at it again, trudging with iron shoes and cast-iron succubus on the back up yet another mountain trail, toward one more rockpile in the sky. If we did it for pay we'd call it slave labor. What punishment could be so cruel and unusual as that which is self-inflicted? And yet, and yet . . . It is not enough to say that we climb a given mountain because no one else has yet done it. Even if true, that is not sufficient. Nor will it do to say, simply, "Somebody has to do it." They won't believe you. Most mountains have now been climbed anyhow, some of them many times. (The trail up Mount Whitney looks, on Labor Day weekends, like a procession of penitents in purgatory, each hiker bearing his cross, bent beneath the weight of an ass's pack of guilt and conscience, toiling upward, upward, ever upward on the stony path, toward the cold bleak summit, through wind, sleet and the thin unnourishing air, threatened at times by fangs of lightning from the gloomy clouds.) Then why? We have not yet answered this question and perhaps no one ever will answer it to the satisfaction of nonclimbers. But one must attempt the answer. "To dare! to dare! ever to dare!" cried Georges Danton in 1792, speaking of revolution but giving us the metaphor we need here. Reproduction and mere survival never has been good enough for humankind. We demand difficulty. Even a simple hike up Whitney, even the mild walk and scramble to the apex of Sierra Blanca in New Mexico (last week's holiday), involves an element of risk. And that's what we want. We love not only the taste of freedom but even more the smell of danger. We take pleasure in the consummation of mental, spiritual, and physical effort in the achievement of the mountain's summit which brings the three together. A banal solution but there is no better; men and women climb mountains—whether in New Hampshire, the Rockies, or the Himalayas—for the same reason they hurl rockets at the moon, launch poems and prayers to the stars, send symphonies of thought, music, mathematics, and fiction into the highest and deepest reaches of the human soul. Because that is our way of imposing our will and the search for apotheosis upon the bland boredom of the universe.

Well, all that rhapsodizing and analyzing accomplishes nothing. Better to drive the car as far up the hill as it will go, climb out, make camp, and breathe in some altitude for a while. My wife and I turned off the highway beyond Ophir, Colorado, near the summit of Lizard Head Pass, 10,000 feet high. We forded a brook, the water clear, and deep as the hubcaps, and drove up an old, rutty, rocky road that leads north toward the peaks. The regular August afternoon rain had begun; the road was slippery and we made only a mile from the pavement before it became impossible to go on. I parked the car under some spruce and fir at the edge of an overgrazed meadow grown up in thistle, dockweed, and skunk cabbage. Not a beautiful meadow, I guess, but there was plenty of firewood, a stream, and a good view of some excellent mountains.

The rain fell softly but steadily and we waited. When it began to slack off I got out and chopped some dry wood from the underside of a log and built a fire. The air did not seem too chilly but my breath vaporized as it floated forth. There was no wind. The blue smoke from the burning chunks of white fir rose straight up into the trees. The clouds broke up a little and the evening sun shone through. Sheep Mountain, above Trout Lake, was lit up suddenly as if by searchlight. Above timberline there were long steep pitches of scree, gray and broken granite; above that, in the cliffs, were bands of iron and manganese oxides giving the San Miguel Mountains a little extra color that most mountains lack, a touch of the exotic and sinister; in the couloirs lay beds of old snow, dusted brown and red by the summer winds; a few icy cornices clung to ridges. Crags, pinnacles, and battlements of rotten rock formed the skyline.

The rain stopped before sundown. My wife cooked supper and I carried
water up from the stream and gathered more wood. The sky cleared
toward the west and north. We could see Mount Wilson emerging from
the clouds. Lizard Head itself became visible, a chimneylike structure
with vertical walls some five hundred feet high.

My objective this time was Wilson Peak, 14,017 feet above sea level.
The previous summer I had tried to climb Mount Wilson, a couple of
hundred feet higher than Wilson Peak and much more rugged. A friend
and I walked up the southwest ridge, in bad weather as usual. We got to
the 13,000-foot level before giving up in the midst of a blizzard. The
visibility was down to thirty feet, we knew nothing about the route ahead,
we had no rope with us, we were cold and hungry and didn't really want
to go on up the mountain that day anyhow.

Two years earlier I had made a half-hearted attempt on Mount Sneffels,
another 14'er in the San Juan Range, and failed that one too, again
turning back some 1,000 feet below the summit. Too much sleet bouncing
off my head, too much lightning bombarding the rocks. One thing that I
like about mountain climbing is that there are always plenty of excuses
available for turning back before disaster strikes. I mean the fatal kind,
death. As it inevitably will anyhow, one of these days—but I don't know
of any better way or place to meet that little mystery than up in the
mountains. Better by far than death in a hospital bed. . . . It seems a
nuisance that the subject of mortality should continually obtrude itself,
when I would much rather talk about silverleaf lupine and blue columbine.
Somehow it keeps coming up, along with the mountain air, the white roar
of the waterfalls, the stillness of timberline, the clarity of the peaks. But
there is nothing depressing or morbid in this. Quite the contrary, it is
the sense of danger which adds to the excitement and joy of being—
despite the enormous odds—still here, walking, kicking, talking. Always
walking and jabbering, that's the essence of this curious animal, this
evoluted beast from the dark lagoon, Man.

The new moon followed the sun down beyond the mountain. We sat for
a while by the fire, sipping at a bottle of cognac, then went to bed early.
August is not the best of months for hiking in the Colorado Alps. Zipped
together in our downy cocoon we watched the stars and clouds, listened
to the tumbling stream, fell off the mountain into dreams.

The morning looked good but I wasted too much time getting started. I
put on fresh socks and threw some jerky and an orange and a parka into
my day pack and started up the old road. My wife accompanied me for a
couple of miles, then veered off to photograph flowers and mushrooms.
This was going to be a solo hike. Renée does not enjoy, or suffer from,
the ridiculous compulsion to keep walking upward until there is no
further upward to walk to.

As always, I found the first part of the ascent painful, myself begrudging
the same old drag of gravity that always seems like blind harassment on
nature's part. But again, as before, the steady plod pays off and something
truly like second wind comes into play, and after a while you forget the
burden of uphill walking and begin to think about better things.

A pair of big brown mule deer, for example, on the far side of a marshy
meadow. I noted them a moment before they spotted me and instinctively
I froze. They shuffled around nervously, unhappy about my presence, but
finally returned to browsing. Just for the fun of it I sank to my knees and
flat on my belly crawled toward a log that shielded me from their
line of sight. I pushed my walking stick like a rifle before me. When I
reached the log I slid my "rifle" very carefully on top of it and raised my
eyes for an easy 100-yard make-believe broadside shot at the nearest doe.
She was gone; I had a glimpse of a black tail and a pale rump vanishing
into the woods, nothing more.

Upward through the forest, under the dark and shaggy spruce, the
tapered spires of the fir. Glens and groves of quaking aspen here and
there. Open meadows bright with yarrow, fireweed, goldenrod, and
sunshine. Already, however, the clouds were beginning to form above,
though the sky had been absolutely clear an hour earlier. The only thing
certain about mountain weather in August is its unpredictability.

Aside from the deer the wildlife was keeping itself scarce. I saw gray
squirrels and chipmunks, the track and scat of coyote along the trail, a
lot of jays, woodpeckers, and Clark's nutcrackers in the trees. At

timberline I flushed a covey of white-tailed ptarmigan; and from among
the rocks the pikas began to whistle at me, and plump rusty-furred
marmots that spend their entire lives in the alpine zone, merely waiting,
one might easily think, for somebody to come along.

The high forest has its special charms but I think I like most the timberline regions. The trees are few and scattered and grow close to the earth.
The world opens up and one begins to understand what we're doing here
after all. Lizard Head butte towers on my right. Above is the pass
between Lizard Head and Cross Mountain, both of them over 13,000 feet;
beyond the pass loom Mount Wilson and Wilson Peak, a pair of fearsome-
looking 14'ers joined to one another by a high col.

The trail leads ever upward, switchbacking through open fields of flowers
shimmering in the wind, shining with color—purple lupine, Indian
paintbrush, scarlet penstemon, skyrocket gilia, bluebell, larkspur,
columbine, monkshood, sunflower, fleabane, chickory, purple aster—all
massed together in an emphatic statement of first principles, that ancient
creed which insists on the primacy of fecundity, an open invitation to
what His Holiness called "the banquet of life." Lewis Mumford has
pointed out that flowers began to appear on earth at the same time the
mammals were taking over from the dying dynasties of the giant reptiles.
The association of flowers and warm-blooded love is more therefore than
only a romantic convention; it is derived from one of the great leaps
forward in the planet's evolutionary history.

"Near the snow, near the sun, in the highest fields"—I thought of Stephen
Spender's lines as I passed the flowers and heard the wind, the sound of
waterfalls, the air like clear music passing across the walls of rock, and
felt the sun blazing down from the violet sky—though already tired,
sweating, hungry, I enjoyed once again the exhilaration of the high
places. Beyond the crest of the pass I sat down on the sunny side of a
rock, out of the wind, and ate my lunch.

Mount Wilson hangs over me on the west, to my way of thinking an
appalling skyscraper of red and gray rock, suspended snowfields, a jumble
of craggy peaks joined by knife-edge ridges of weathered and shattered
stone. Wilson Peak, its lesser mate, looks more reasonable, despite a
sprinkling of fresh snow along its sides. That snow lies deep in the
cracks and crevices that zigzag lightning-style up the mountain's flanks.
From the summit of the pass it was necessary to descend a thousand feet
or so into the classic U-shaped glacial cirque of Bilk Creek. I walked down
the trail, reluctant to give up so much hard-earned elevation, but the
only alternative would have been an up-and-down scramble across the
loose rock on the slopes of Cross Mountain and Mount Wilson. Good
ankle-sprain and cartilage-twist country.

Down in the drainage basin I crossed the creek and resumed the upward
trudge, following the cobbled remains of an old mining road. I was still
well above timberline. To the northeast I could see Sneffels and the other
peaks that rise above Telluride and Ouray. Clouds were gathering around
them, fleets and armadas of dazzling white. Down below I saw two hikers
with backpacks descending the trail along Bilk Creek, in retreat. There
is a general rule: get off the peaks by one o'clock. The sun was now
noon-high. Even so, it still shone on me, plenty of open sky remained,
and I thought, with a little luck in the weather, that I might make it to
the top before the storm began.

Plodding upward over the rock, I had to pause every twenty or thirty
paces for a bit of a blow. I was in less than good shape, hauling my
summertime belly, my flat feet and my irritable, uncontrolled brain up
this absurd bulge of granite. How much more sensible, I thought, to be
back in camp, sitting on a log, drinking sweet green Coors out of a
can, watching my wife (bless her) cooking up some kind of slumgullion
stew in the old Dutch oven. These treacherous thoughts did not occupy
much of my time or slow my pace. I kept going, trying to avoid the
streams of water running among the stones of the trail, coming from
melting snowbanks, gushing from caves in the hollowed ice.

In the upper basin I passed three shallow lakes, immaculate and perfect
bodies of water, emerald green when viewed from the trail, a turquoise
blue from above. Cascades tumbled through gorges in the rock, disappearing beneath the talus, the scree, the wreckage of the mountains, and
re-emerging as brooks at the head of the lakes. Almost everything in

sight was either stone or water, as in the beginning, but there were a
few clumps of green among the boulder fields, miniature pastures of grass
and turf where the pikas make their living. Rock and grass, water and
snow, all glittered under the sun, through the pellucid air, with that
vibrant perfection which is characteristic of desert, seashore, and high
mountain scenes. Almost too perfect; I should have brought along
a few beer cans to litter about, give the place a natural look.

So much for aesthetics. Time for haste. The clouds are mating and
amalgamating, a certain poisonous-looking mist floats across the east
face of Mount Wilson, and I still have a couple of miles to go, a couple of
thousand feet to climb. The trail leads up beside the cascades, traverses
the slopes of reposing scree and crosses a firm and dusty snowfield.
I'm up in the world of broken stone, sliding rock, frozen snow. Life,
however, continues even here. I see little black spiders with gray
abdomens scuttle over the stone, and rosy finches, busy at something,
flitting low over the scree, alighting, taking off.

A giant shadow passes over me, a chill touches my skin, and I notice
snowflakes, genuine August snowflakes, delicate, whimsical, and
ephemeral, floating on the air. Thunder in the distance. A big lid is closing
off the sky, although to the east past Lizard Head, where a segment of
rainbow hangs from the clouds, I can still see blue. The drifting snowflakes are followed by a drizzle of rain; retreat for shelter to an old cabin
at the 12,000-foot level, the remains of some gold miner's shack. I wait
there, nibbling on jerky but the rain continues. I put on my parka and
go outside. The clouds are moving across the sky so fast that it seems
possible the weather may clear again.

The trail leads up to the saddle or col between the two great peaks. I am
determined to get at least that far and have a look at the weather coming
in from the northwest. I plod up a snowfield, kicking steps as I go, up
more loose rock, following the dim vestige of a path, and reach the col.
I look down the other side at more red and gray rockslides, fields of snow,
alpine lakes, old test-holes and miners' diggings. But the sky looks
unfavorable, with mountains of black writhing clouds storming my way,
trailing curtains of sleet, rain, and snow, rumbling with thunder. I look
up. The peaks are already socked in, hidden from sight though no more
at most than a thousand feet above me.

Shall I go on? I feel exhausted, but I always feel that way at 13,000; I
know my rubbery legs well enough to know that from here on up it is a
matter of mind as well as muscle, that I have the power to decide on
victory or defeat (again), triumph or ignominy. The attack, the assault,
can be carried if the determination is present. *Now or never.*

But I can't see a thing up there except purling vapors. The wind is
whistling over the pass, my ears are aching from the cold, while pellets
of frozen snow patter on my hood, gathering in clusters on the rocks. The
rock will soon be wet and slippery. Nor do I like the sound of that thunder
coming closer. A lightning storm can develop on these peaks in minutes.
"Remember Mallory!" I tell myself, summoning a little inspiration and
courage. (Irvine too!) "Okay," I reply, "I remember." He disappeared into
eternity, becoming a legend. Do I want to become a legend? Well, yes, of
course—but not yet. Good. I turn around. A victory for ignominy, I
descend the rocks, glissade the snowfield, retreat to Bilk Creek and tramp
up to Lizard Head and down the other side to camp, five miles away,
while the storm blows over, the sky clears and the sun comes out, and
I realize that I might have done it after all. That I almost did.

What does it matter? The mountain is still there, waiting for me. I'll be
back next year. All of those mountains out there, all around the world,
tall and absurd and splendid, waiting for us. That is the good part.

Telluride, Colorado
August 1975

The Mountains
of Alaska

The Alaska mountains are a wilderness of rock, snow, tundra, mountain
meadows, volcanoes, glaciers, and rain-born forests. They sprawl in their
many ranges, valleys, and isolated peaks across an area wider than the
continental United States. In length, their territory stretches from the
Canadian border to the Gulf of Mexico. They conform to no orderly
pattern. They are patched and strewn about in a variety of landscapes.
The mountains curve out to sea for more than a thousand miles, forming
the Aleutian Islands. They run down the Alaskan Panhandle, flanking
the Yukon and British Columbia, and give the coast noble and somber
contrast with the Pacific.
The great Brooks Range stands north of all the mountains, an east-west
complex that runs almost the full width of northern Alaska,protecting
central Alaska from the rigors of the Arctic. Due south of it, lying
across the mid-southern section of the state, is the Alaska Range,
containing North America's highest peak, Mount McKinley. The height
of McKinley came from an upthrust scores of millions of years ago, but
the Aleutian volcanoes, more than eighty of them, are born of recent
volcanism, some of it occurring within the past century.
The Chugach Mountains begin the coast ranges. Behind them, the
Wrangell Mountains lead southeast to the St. Elias Mountains,which
run directly into the Fairweather Range. At the end of the
Fairweathers is Glacier Bay, a deep inlet cut behind the coast
mountains and bordering more mountains inland.
Almost nothing unifies these mountains except the size of the territory
they cover. Unlike the Himalayas, which are quite uniform in appearance,
the changes in mood, form, atmosphere, altitude, and size make the
Alaska mountain experience an ever-changing sequence of surprises. At
the thick base of the Alaska Peninsula, before it tapers into the
Aleutian Islands, there is a concentration of fire, chaotic with recent
eruption—Katmai. There, in June, 1912, a sixty-hour eruption created a
new volcano, Novarupta, which destroyed an entire valley, hurled 33
million tons of rock out of the earth, and left behind the Valley of Ten
Thousand Smokes, a steaming wilderness of vapor holes, fallen pumice
and ash piled hundreds of feet deep.
Katmai displays the essence of the Alaskan mountain experience: it
contains both the destruction of violent geological activity and the
luxuriant growth that marks coastal mountains. It includes both areas
of utter lifelessness, where only ash and pumice and steam rule the
surface, and regions of abundant wildlife. Here roam the largest bears
on earth; here are thickly forested mountains, cut by deep valleys.
To reconcile this landscape with any part of the cold, barren Brooks
Range is impossible. The Brooks, which is actually a part of the Rocky
Mountain system, consists of wild and rugged mountains that give an
object lesson in geology. The spines of granite still show the marks of

their resistance to the smothering glaciers of the Pleistocene. The ridges, cliffs, peaks, towers, and precipices are still continually breaking down in small explosions of splintered rock under the influences of 100-degree-below-zero temperatures.

Both the Brooks and the Aleutians are homes to bad weather. But the Brooks receive the full impact of Arctic cold and wind, whereas the Aleutians are mostly shrouded in fogs created by chill Siberian winds and cold Bering Sea currents meeting masses of warm air and warm water moving northeast across the Pacific.

Merely to explore the Alaskan mountains has, from the eighteenth century, taxed man's best efforts. The Brooks Range was not circumnavigated until the 1930s. The Alaska Range was not traversed until the 1950s. The Aleutians were more accessible, but they were still the last parts of the habitable world to be explored by Europeans. Vitus Bering, a Dane serving in the Russian navy, reached the Aleutians in 1741. He was less interested in the native Aleuts than in the immense populations of seals and foxes, seabirds, and, particularly, sea otters. Thus while the desolate Brooks offered only thin pickings to early trappers seeking skins, the Aleutians ultimately yielded millions of dollars in skins to greedy Russian exploiters. They were followed by equally rapacious American hunters after the purchase of the Alaska territories from Russia in 1867.

The coast ranges, on the other hand, were always relatively accessible, and they express an especially dramatic quality of the Alaska mountains. In places, only two or three thousand years ago, the present landscapes were entirely covered with ice. Scenes of great chaos abound where the destruction by ice has not been mended by time. Huge piles of moraine lie about, dumped by glaciers which have now partially retreated into the mountains; and trees establish themselves on still shifting material in many of the inlets of Glacier Bay.

More ice and snow may lie in the coastal region than on all the rest of the mountains in the world put together. The Himalayas do not get nearly the precipitation of snow that these sharply uplifted mountains, some of them rising directly from the sea, receive from Pacific Ocean moisture. One glacier is nearly as big as the state of Delaware.

Here, too, more contrasts: below the icefields the shoreline forests are green and majestic, flourishing under the heavy rain falling on these coasts. So pristine is this region that 30,000 bald eagles nest in its refuge, patroling the inlets and foothills, the mountains and glaciers. The Alaska mountains dazzle the eye of mountain lover and casual traveler alike. No man seeing the diversity of their forms, the height of their peaks, the size of their forests and glaciers, can ever feel the same way again about the earth he lives on.

Brooks Range

One of the most dramatic collisions of the earth's elements occurs in the Arrigetch Peaks, which are part of the massive Brooks Range of Alaska. The Eskimos, observing these towering spires of granite, said they looked like the extended fingers of a giant, and their word for this—*arrigetch*—matches the raw landscape. But while an Eskimo can relate these spires to a titan's fingers, it is an image that sits uncomfortably on the non-Eskimo mind.

Trapped within these somber peaks is the Arrigetch Valley, a perfect, jewel-like haven for animal and plant life. Travelers with strength and determination enough to reach the valley are given a Jules Verne view of the wilderness. The scree of broken mountains tumbles down in long, graceful slides to an enclosed tundra world, where dwarf willows, grasses, sedges, and delicate Arctic flowers grow.

To this day, the Brooks remain enigmatic and difficult to explore. Although it contains many low eroded ranges which contradict much of its starkness, its atmosphere is hostile. The peak of Igikpak is typical of the Arrigetch region and much of the Brooks. It stands like a roughly chiseled skyscraper, its last 200 feet unbroken vertical pillars of granite, one capped by thirty feet of overhang. Igikpak was not climbed until 1968.

The Brooks Range is flung six hundred miles across the northern half of Alaska, 200 miles wide, and covers 156,000 square miles. It is the northernmost major range of mountains in the world, a complex inter-locking of dozens of different mountain systems and valleys, of high plateaus and lakes locked in ice, of thin taiga woodlands and sweeping tundra valleys and of steep-sided peaks stabbing many horizons.

An American government geologist, Philip Smith, reached the Arrigetch Valley in 1911, but it was another eleven years before Adolph and Olaus Murie, two biologists famous for their work on wolves, circled the entire range in an epic journey. During the 1930s, Robert Marshall, who seems to have been more interested in exploring the unknown than in measuring tree growth as he had planned, walked more of the Brooks than any man before him, and mapped much of the range.

The Brooks Range rose from the Arctic Ocean more than 100 million years ago. During the Pleistocene, great sheets of advancing and retreating ice cut and shaped the range into its present form. Ice gouged out valleys with steep, almost vertical sides. Ice ground hard ridges into the shapes of massive ax blades. It scored valley walls with long slashes which are still visible. It dug holes that would become mountain lakes.

The climate of the range creates atmospheres of violence. Short summers, with unpredictable weather, see much activity crammed into six or seven weeks of above-freezing weather. When clouds move in from the Chukchi Sea, the mountains dance with the changing light. The sun pierces masses of black rushing mist to highlight the bare, erosion-ravaged mountain slopes with a golden glow.

Staining the sides of mountains are faint touches of green which indicate that there are plants living close to its many rocky peaks. Reindeer moss and sphagnum decorate the summer tundra, while yellow blooms of Arctic poppy nod in the cool winds. Lupines flourish, along with Labrador tea, elephant head, and shooting star.

More than a quarter of a million caribou winter in the shelter of the range. The main herd comes south from the northern tundra slopes. Some of these animals drive deeply into the range through the basin of the Noatak River, which runs east to west. The river drains a long, narrow territory which includes the melting glaciers on Mount Igikpak.

At the eastern end of the range, the Sheenjek Valley provides a touch of warmth amid austerity. Red squirrels whisk up stunted spruce, grayling flourish in the waters, and some summer days are twenty degrees warmer here than the forty-five-degree average for the entire range. Loons call from Last Lake in the valley, their cry exactly suited to this "perfect lonely land," as one traveler described it.

If there is a word to match the Brooks, it is aloofness. Perhaps this is due to the quality of the light, which on clear days has a special Arctic clarity that reveals every detail of the landscape with piercing realism. It is this quality of aloofness that distinguishes the Brooks from the ranges south of it, the Alaska Range, the coast ranges, and the Aleutian Island, which stretch hundreds of miles out into the north Pacific.

15. Two glaciers, grinding out depressions on either side, created this ridge called an arête. The action of the ice did much to shape the Brooks Range.
(Philip Vaughan)

16. The sweeping panoramas of the Arrigetch Valley so impressed explorer Robert Marshall that he named it the Arctic Yosemite when he was laboriously trekking through the Brooks Range early in this century. Such magnificent scenery is typical of a new national park in the area, the Gates of the Arctic.
(Robert Belous)

20. The Noatak River, fed by glaciers on Mount Igikpak, has created a large river basin in its wandering passage to the Chukchi Sea just north of the Arctic Circle. Flowing south of the Brooks Range, the Noatak is crossed by one of Alaska's largest caribou herds, about a quarter of a million animals, on its way to winter shelter and grazing. *(M. Woodbridge Williams)*

18. The two spires of Mount Igikpak, at 8,510 feet, make this the tallest mountain in the western Brooks Range and one of the most spectacular. The Eskimos named it "Two Big Peaks." Its vertical column walls, 200 feet high and capped by overhanging rock, are a major mountaineering challenge. *(David Roberts)*

19. Arrigetch means "fingers extended" in Eskimo, and the angular jumble of rocks in which glacial lakes are trapped make this a place of rugged beauty. The main track of the glacier now holds a wandering stream. *(Robert Belous)*

Alaska Range

The Russian explorer Ivan Petroff, sailing the coasts of Alaska in 1880, reported that there were "stories of mountains of immense altitudes, visible for hundreds of miles . . . what the country north of Cook Inlet is like no civilized man can tell, as in all the years of occupation of the Coast by the Caucasian race, it has remained a sealed book." Petroff was undoubtedly referring to the Alaska Range, since the other big ranges in Alaska were visible from the sea.

For more than a century, the Alaska Range, swinging in a giant 600-mile curve across the middle of the state to the Alaska Peninsula, was considered impassable. The Russians, despite their long occupation of the coastal parts of Alaska, apparently saw the largest peak, 20,320-foot Mount McKinley—the highest peak in North America, called Denali or "The Great One" by the Indians—as an impassable mountain locked behind the barrier of the rest of the range.

But by the end of the nineteenth century, men were ready to test the fastness of the Alaska Range. In 1898, a geologist, Arthur E. Spurr, led an expedition that traveled 1,425 miles between May 7 and October 31, in an epic exploration of Alaskan territory. Plagued by confusing terrain and treacherous conditions, he nevertheless completely traversed the range. He inspired a U. S. Army team to try to duplicate his effort the following year, but even with the experiences of the Spurr party available to them, the army expedition took 167 days to tramp 1,000 miles. The men were abandoned by their guides, and they almost died of starvation.

Actually, the Alaska Range, while difficult and dangerous, is dwarfed by the size of its central massif—Mount McKinley and its satellite peaks. The rest of the range's mountains are not spectacularly high. Still, these peaks—and there are hundreds of them—offer the human traveler no easy access. When, in 1964, two Harvard students, David Roberts and Don Jensen, challenged the mountaineering problems of a relatively small peak, 12,540-foot Mount Deborah in the Hayes Range about fifty miles east of McKinley National Park, they found the climbing was so tough that they were exhausted most of the time, and numbed by bitter cold. They had to traverse knife-edged ridges of snow, a common phenomenon throughout the range. Twice they fell into crevasses, another common danger. An earthquake struck.

As they neared the top, Roberts paused to look upward. "Above, blocking out half the sky, was the terrible black cliff, the 600-foot wall that we had once so blithely, back in Cambridge, allowed three days to climb. At its upper rim, nearly a thousand feet above me, hovered monstrous chunks of ice, like aimed cannons at the top of a castle wall. As I watched, one broke off, then smashed violently on a ledge to my left and bounced out of sight down the precipice. I had never seen a mountain . . . so numbing, so haunted with impossibility and danger."

Already defeated in their minds, Roberts and Jensen finally could not go on. In addition to all the other horrors, the rock had become so rotten that further climbing would have been suicidal.

The Alaska Range is relatively young. Its last uplift began only two million years ago and is still going on. Earthquakes frequently dislodge immense masses of rock. Even the summers are treacherous. A beautiful, cool, balmy day can abruptly turn bitter cold, when a July blizzard sweeps through parts of the range.

The great quantities of snow that fall in places do not make the country easy to traverse. Precipitation of up to 160 inches is common enough, along with temperatures that drop to fifty below zero. The range is threaded with icy streams and rivers, each appearing to have a different personality. The melting waters of glaciers make the East Fork of the Toklat River boil as it roars through a canyon.

But there is a gentle counterpoint to all this harshness. The foothills sparkle with ponds. Tundra rolls green across the bare rock. The slopes blaze with wildflowers. The marmot's whistle echoes in high places. Grizzlies fish the streams. Caribou trudge through the valleys and over the foothills. The skimpy stands of black spruce and white spruce hold moose and porcupines.

Yet Petroff's "mountains of immense altitudes" dominate every view, testifying to the harshness of the Alaska Range and the isolation of soaring McKinley standing remotely behind the outer defenses of the inhospitable range.

23. The great Alaska Range has many unnamed peaks. This one, rising 8,520 feet in the Cathedral Spires, is part of the Kichatna Mountains about seventy miles southwest of Mount McKinley. (David Roberts)

24. A violent August storm envelops the foothills near Polychrome Pass in McKinley National Park. Such weather often brings snow in July and has, over the centuries, caused massive erosion throughout the Alaska Range. (Harald Sund)

26. The starkness of the Alaska Range is softened in mid-summer by an emerald-green blanket of tundra growth, here covering the range's foothills near Thorofare Pass in Mount McKinley National Park. (Willis Peterson)

Mount McKinley

Bradford Washburn, a mountaineer and a notable scientist who was one of the first men to explore the Alaska Range, quickly became entranced by the special quality of these mountains. "A peak of 20,000 feet," he said, referring to Mount McKinley, "is of no great importance in the Andes, far less in the Himalayas, where almost a thousand summits outrank McKinley. Yet this mountain has held a particular fascination for me over a long period of years and its ascent, exploration and mapping have been one of my prime interests."

Mount McKinley, which has two peaks, one about 800 feet lower than the other, is literally enthroned in glaciers. Seen from a very high aerial position, the glaciers radiate away from the mountain in all directions. They twist and turn, branch and rebranch like a network of veins. They are one reason why access to McKinley was for so long considered to be almost impossible.

The great Muldrow Glacier runs east and west along the northern fringe of the McKinley complex, then branches sharply into a valley north of the range. The Kahiltna, a massive outpouring from the region of Mount Crosson, just west of McKinley, runs almost due south, as does the Ruth Glacier, south of McKinley.

The controversial Arctic explorer Frederick A. Cook, claimed to have climbed Mount McKinley early in the century, and published a detailed account of the ascent, with pictures. But when two Alaska prospectors, William Taylor and Pete Anderson, climbed one of the twin summits in 1910, their descriptions did not tally with Cook's, and a picture he published of himself at the summit appeared to be fraudulent. But he did widely explore the approaches to the mountain, and gave some of the more revealing descriptions of the difficulties of functioning in the Alaska Range.

"The area of this mountain is far inland, in the heart of most difficult and trackless country, making the transportation of man and supplies a very arduous task," wrote Cook. "The thick underbrush, the endless marshes, and the myriads of vicious mosquitoes, bring to the traveler the troubles of the tropics; the necessity of fording and swimming icy streams, the almost perpetual cold rains, the camps in high altitudes on glaciers, in snows and violent storms, bring to the traveler all of the discomforts of the Arctic explorer; the very difficult slopes, combined with high altitude effects, add to the troubles of the worst Alpine climbs."

The first successful ascent of the highest peak of McKinley was actually made in the middle of 1913 when it was discovered that the Taylor-Anderson climb had only reached the lower summit. The Episcopal arch-deacon of the Yukon, Reverend Hudson Stuck and a companion succeeded because of the lessons learned from the failed expeditions of 1903, 1906, 1910, and 1912. But the climbing conditions were terrible. No further summit attempts were made until 1932, when Allen Carpe, then America's greatest mountaineer, tried McKinley with Theodore Koven. Both died in falls into deep crevasses. In 1954, Elton Thayer, a McKinley Park ranger, reached the highest peak but he, too, was killed in a terrifying 1,000-foot slide near the Muldrow Glacier.

The McKinley region is thus emblematic of the entire range. It has been called "a land of little sticks and tiny flowers," the product of life's adaptation to the long and difficult winters. The winters are so tough that only inches of topsoil are able to thaw during the short summers.

McKinley and the rest of the range offer an unimpaired wilderness. The migrations of the caribou, often moving in herds of thousands across the tundra, thread their way through the high mountain passes en route to winter and summer grazing.

In the lowlands, the grizzly bears fish along the river banks, dig roots and consume berries on the mountain slopes, and hunt ground squirrels in their burrows among the rocks. Ravens and magpies and gray jays join them in scavenging scraps left by other hunters. In the ponds and streams, waterfowl breed and beavers build their dams and lodges.

It is all stunningly beautiful and rugged country. When Bradford Washburn reached the summit of Mount McKinley, it was a rare clear day, and he got a view spread across 100,000 miles. He summed up the experience of the Alaska Range in one phrase. He said the view from McKinley was "like looking out of the very windows of heaven."

29. Deep shadows form on McKinley's cold and forbidding summit at twilight. Wintertime winds of 100 miles an hour, temperatures of 60 degrees below zero, and the nearly four-mile altitude make this one of the most inhospitable places on earth.

30. Winds of near hurricane force sweep powdered snow across the twin peaks of Mount McKinley, which flank the enormous Harper Glacier. In the foreground the steep Karstens Ridge forms the major route to the summit from the northeast.

32. The massive bulk of Mount McKinley, 20,320 feet high, dominates the Alaska Range in splendid isolation, rising 18,000 feet from level lowlands. Even in midsummer the top 16,000 feet of McKinley is covered with snow. In this northeastern view the floodplain of Clearwater Creek fills the foreground.

34. Mount Huntington provides a technical challenge to mountaineers far greater than that of Mount McKinley. Its knife-edged ridges and sheer granite cliffs have already claimed the life of one young climber.
(Bradford Washburn)

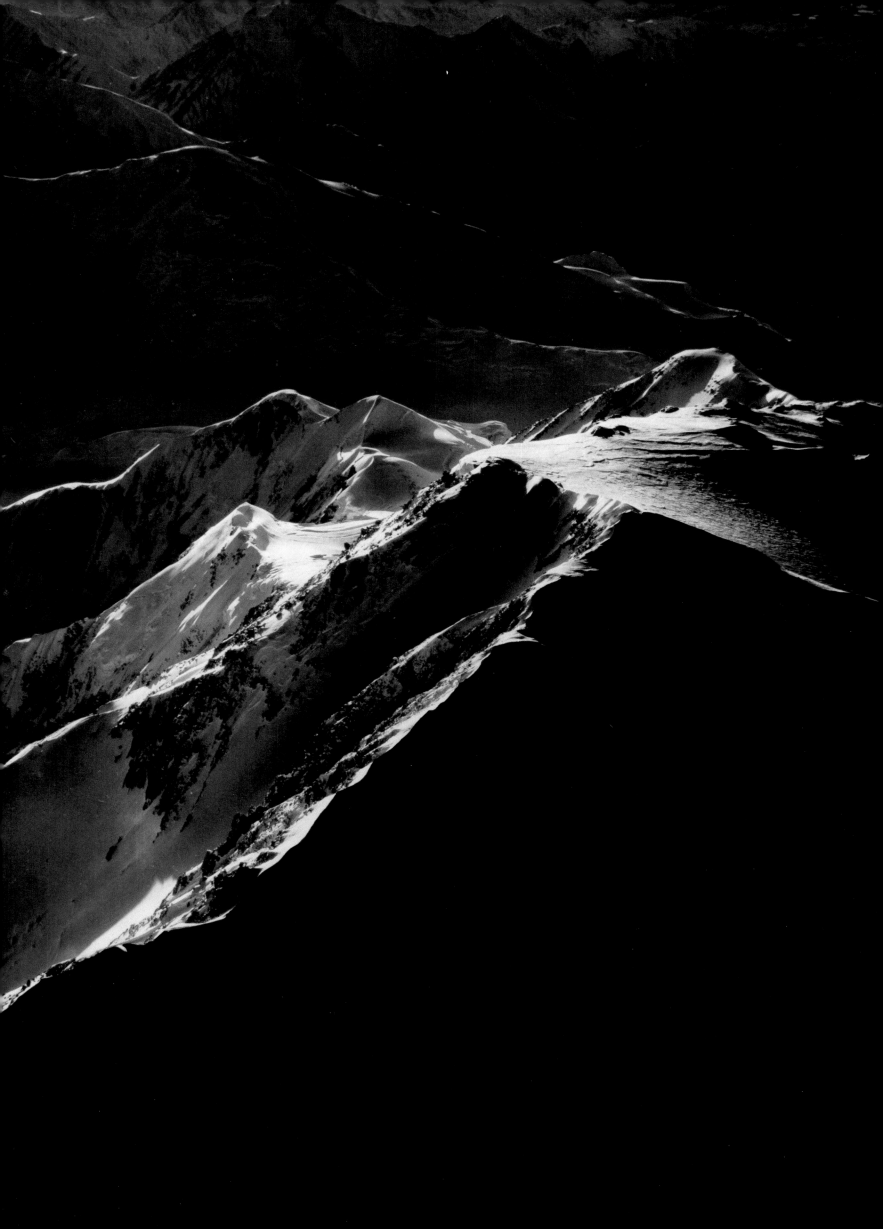

Aleutians

The young and relatively low volcanic mountains of the Aleutians, patched 1,600 miles across the Pacific in a wide arc, lie directly in the turbulent storm track of the north Pacific. The gales are savage, the rains torrential. Only grasses, wild flowers, and crouching shrubs thrive in such a climate. Usually fewer than forty clear days illuminate the islands in a year. The rest of the time winds, rains and almost constant fogs shroud the Aleutians in a north Pacific pall.

The violence and desolation that mark these islands are combined in the unchallenged force of wind and rain smashing into mountains rising directly from the sea, stark, powerful monuments to a volcanic age that is still active. Brooding volcanoes, some still trailing smoke, rise from most of the islands. Makushin, Vsevidof, Round Top, Shishaldin, Bogoslof, Paclof, Korovin, and Isanotski are a few of the larger ones.

The essence of the Aleutians can be seen in the example of one mountain. A small island, twenty-two miles north of Unmak, one of the major islands of the chain, first exploded out of the sea in a huge eruption in 1796. Named Bogoslof by the Russians, it is today the top of a submerged volcano, eight miles in diameter and built up steadily in eruptions that occurred regularly from 1883 into the 1920s and pushed up Bogoslof to its present height of about 5,000 feet.

The mountain is linked, volcanically, to the great eruption of 1912 at Katmai, an area which straddles the thick base of the Alaska Peninsula. There, with the Buttress Range backing the Valley of Ten Thousand Smokes, and with the solid plug of magma blocking the crater of the new volcano, Novarupta, harsh testimony to the power of volcanism is still visible. Tons of pumice and ash hurled into the air by the eruption spread throughout the northern hemisphere, causing brilliant sunsets in North America, Europe, and Asia for several years.

Earthquakes regularly shake the area with jolts that would wreck cities. A quake in 1964 moved some of the mountains more than fifty feet. It dropped their peaks by ten feet or more. Montagu Island, fifty miles long, was lifted thirty feet and tilted. Forests were flattened by hurricane-force winds ripping along the shoreline. A tidal wave, born of the quake, sped out into the Pacific at 430 miles an hour.

Neither the Aleuts nor the Russians—who enslaved, exploited, and eventually reduced the original Aleut population from 25,000 to 2,000—were much interested in the monumental grandeur of the conical peaks rising above them. They may have been impressed by the austere beauty of Mount Shishaldin, which, at 9,387 feet, is the largest mountain in the chain, rising from the center of Unimak island, the biggest island and the closest one to the Alaskan mainland.

The continuous plume of volcanic steam rolling away from its summit in the great winds—it is also called Smoking Moses—may have caused some apprehension, neither Russian nor Aleut understanding that even plants and animals used the volcanic mountains for their homes.

Mountain and man still live close together, but it is the plants and animals, which have conquered the mountains. On the second largest Aleutian island, Unalaska, some sixty-seven miles long, the short growing season lasts from July to early September. Meadows around Mount Makushin, 5,000 feet, are smothered with masses of white-flowered narcissus anemones. Grasses and sedges pack together, and purple wild geraniums, asters and lupines bloom in the chill damp air.

As the Aleutians curve west toward Japan, the volcanoes diminish and the islands thin out and decrease in size, just as they do in the Hawaiian archipelago, far to the south. Finally, Amchitka Island, in the Rat Islands, is the only non-mountainous island in the chain.

As a result of Bering's explorations in the eighteenth century, the Russians learned that the islands of the north Pacific were rich in seals, foxes, and, most particularly, sea otters. Bering eventually died of scurvy, but his men brought back 900 sea-otter skins and began the race to exploit the Aleutians which continued right until the beginning of the twentieth century. Then the Americans, appalled at their own slaughter of seals, otters, and seabirds, began a program of conservation. By that time, only a few thousand Aleuts remained; the seals and otters were cut to shadows of their old numbers. The Aleutians then began a process of recovery, which continues today, to become one of the great repositories of wildlife anywhere on earth.

37. Patches of snow edge a small cinder cone on the floor of Aniakchak Caldera in the Alaska Peninsula section of the Aleutian Mountain Range.

38. The Aleutians embody the violence of volcanic genesis. The rim of the vast Aniakchak Caldera is more than six miles wide and contains within its 4,000-foot-high walls warm springs, cinder cones, and a large lake. Caribou, grizzly bears, eagles, and many other kinds of wildlife roam the crater's floor. *(M. Woodbridge Williams)*

40. A circular volcanic plug set in a small crater marks the final act of the famed Novarupta Volcano eruption of June 6, 1912. The explosion hurled 33 million tons of rock into the air, spread ash over 42,000 square miles, and winds blew the volcanic dust all around the northern hemisphere. It created the steaming Valley of Ten Thousand Smokes, now contained in the Katmai National Monument.

41. The explosion of Novarupta laid down a blanket of ash and pumice in some places more than 300 feet deep. Fed by meltwater from thawing glaciers, the turbulent River Lethe has cut its way through the volcano's debris. Snowcapped Mount Mageik and Mount Martin, in the background, are among the highest peaks in the Aleutian Range. *(Harald Sund)*

42. These tumbled landscapes of jagged rocks are nearly all the work of ancient volcanoes where the Aleutian Range joins the mainland. Here, among unnamed valleys, a once great mountain is now worn down to a spectacular tusk at Merrill Pass near Lake Clark in the Northern Aleutians. *(Keith Trexler)*

Coast Ranges

The Panhandle of Alaska lies close to the Japan Current and a constant flow of warm wet air is driven from the sea far inland. It hits the coast mountains, rises rapidly, and its moisture is turned into torrents of rain and snow. Some of the Panhandle gets up to fifteen feet of precipitation a year. This produces a warmer, moister environment in which lofty forests of western hemlock and Sitka spruce grow. The large snowfalls produce glaciers which stream out of the highest parts of the coast ranges.

A Russian, Alexis Tchikov, in 1741, was the first European to see these coastal mountains. He did not sight the Chugach Mountains, the most westerly of the coast ranges, which almost reach the conjunction of the Alaska Range and the beginning of the Aleutian Range. The Chugach Mountains are so rugged that even today most of their peaks have not been climbed. Northeast of them lie the inland Wrangell Mountains leading into the St. Elias Mountains which extend to the south. But Tchikov did see the Fairweathers, which, as the highest and most heavily snow-struck coastal mountains in the world, gave him a sobering first view of the American continent. He did not explore the coast systematically, so he did not understand that this great range, up to forty miles wide, plunged southward to its meeting with the icefield-riddled peninsula that enclosed Glacier Bay.

Captain James Cook followed Tchikov thirty-seven years later on the *Resolution* and he was not even aware of the existence of Glacier Bay lying behind the Fairweathers. Instead, he contented himself with a log note concerning "a fine gale at northeast and clear weather," unusual enough for the time and place.

Vitus Bering was powerfully impressed by giant Mount St. Elias, 18,008 feet, largest mountain of the St. Elias Range which lies immediately to the north of Fairweathers. It dwarfs all the other coast range mountains, but it exemplifies their form. Its broad majestic glaciers flow into the sea, breaking off as giant icebergs that lie, craggy and blue, in the sheltered inlets.

Glacier Bay is not at the end of the coast ranges, but it is a visual terminus: nothing so grand is seen anywhere farther south along the coast. It is a monument both to an ice age recently past and to the rapid retreat of the ice during the present age of thaw. When Captain George Vancouver sailed through Icy Inlet in 1794, Glacier Bay was almost totally choked with ice. Vancouver did not even know that it was an inlet. All he could see was a mountainous wall of ice facing him, the termination of the glacier that completely filled Glacier Bay. No fewer than 100,000 square miles of almost unbroken ice lay before him. His ship stood at the end of the Fairweather Range, in the lea of such snow giants as Mount Quincy Adams, 13,850 feet; Mount Fairweather, 15,390 feet; Mount Crillon, 12,728 feet; and many other smaller mountains. In places the ice was then 4,000 feet thick.

Today the ice has retreated an average of forty miles, opening up Glacier Bay's sixty-mile length, and giving separate identity to a host of glaciers—La Perouse, which reaches the sea on the western side; Brady, which comes out of the 1,000-square-mile Brady icefield; Margerie; Reid; Hugh Miller; and, on the eastern side of the Bay, Carroll Glacier, Casement, McBride, Muir, Riggs, and Grand Pacific at the head of the bay. Although it is only a little more than 120 years since Vancouver's visit, the plants have reclaimed land once owned by the glaciers.

John Muir penetrated the deepest inlet of Glacier Bay to reach Grand Pacific Glacier where, after witnessing the "unveiling of the majestic peaks and glaciers in their baptism in the down-pouring sunbeams", he could not believe that he would ever see anything finer in nature.

But the next morning, he wakened to "the thunder of newborn bergs." Then, as his party prepared to move he saw the dawn. "We were startled by the sudden appearance of a red light burning with a strange unearthly splendor on the topmost peak of the Fairweather Mountains . . . it spread and spread until the whole range down to the level of the glaciers was filled with celestial fire . . . indescribably rich and deep . . . we stood awestricken, gazing at the holy vision; and had we seen the heavens opened and God made manifest, our attention could not have been more tremendously strained."

45. An Ice Age monument, its glaciers tumbling down between bare walls of rock, stands in a wreath of mist in the Wrangell Mountains. Part of Alaska's coast ranges, they form one of the largest masses of high mountains in the United States. *(M. Woodbridge Williams)*

46. The mighty Juneau icefield in the Alaska Coast Mountains covers 1,500 square miles and is the source of over 100 glaciers. Here, less than thirty miles north of Juneau, the Antler peaks overlook Hades Highway and East Twin Glacier. *(Jim Stuart)*

48. Icebergs break away from the majestic Portage Glacier flowing down from the Chugach Mountains on the Kenai Peninsula. Great mountains, sheltered inlets, and massive glaciers give this coastal region of Alaska an unchallenged dignity and beauty. *(Robert Belous)*

50. The lofty Fairweather Range flanks Bartlett Cove, in Glacier Bay National Monument, north of Juneau. At dusk, the blended colors of sky and water bathe the peaks—some of which rise above 15,000 feet—in rich hues. *(Harald Sund)*

The Canadian Rockies

The Canadian Rockies are deceptive. They appear just as impressive, both in height and scope, as the Colorado Rockies. Yet they are not nearly as big as the mountains farther south. When they are approached from the featureless prairies of Canada, their sudden emergence magnifies them in the eyes and imaginations of men. David Thompson, an explorer working with the Northwest Company, who helped pioneer fur-trading posts on the Pacific coast in the early 1800s, thought the two great peaks flanking the Athabaska Pass—mountains later known as Mount Brown and Mount Hooker—to be at least 18,000 feet high—nearly as tall as Mount McKinley in Alaska—when, in fact, neither exceeds 12,000 feet.

When a Scottish botanist, David Douglas, ventured into this mountain country in 1827, he believed Mount Brown and Mount Hooker to be the highest mountains yet found in North America. The mistake made by Thompson and Douglas is understandable. Both mountains are located in a landscape so grandiose that they loom larger than reality.

Raymond Patterson, an explorer, was traveling in the Canadian Rockies in the area of the White River divide when he noted this deceptiveness. "High in the air there was a mist of fine snow through which the sun was now struggling. Seen through this drifting, glittering haze the peaks of Mount Cadorna looked twice their real height. Glaciers swept down from them, disappearing into the old forest at the head of Cadorna Lake. The three veiled peaks seemed to lean forward; it was as if they were reaching towards us . . . with chill fingers of ice."

To the natural grandeur of the Canadian Rockies must be added an ever present atmosphere of surprise. Each new turn in each valley brings astonishment. The peaks themselves are sculpted in such a variety of forms that they have a different atmosphere from the mountains of Montana or the Colorado Rockies.

Patterson was traveling beyond the Elk Trail Pass, moving through grand scenery, when he was struck by one of the many surprises of the Canadian mountains. ". . . as the summit of the hill opened up, we saw that it was one living, shimmering carpet of many colours; here, by God's truth, were flowers beyond all imagining—flowers such as we had never seen. It was the kingdom of the flowers, the garden of the gods."

The Canadian Rocky Mountains are a part of the great complex of ranges, valleys, and lakes that run down the mountain spine of western North America. A relative intimacy of scale pervades them, created by a series of spectacular juxtapositions of great peaks and verdant valleys. These characteristic scenes are repeated through much of their area; a serene and picturesque foreground of a mirror lake with its sculpted groves of trees, flower-filled meadows, and tiny waterfalls dropping into tarns set against a backdrop of massive chunks of bare rock rising to neck-twisting heights.

52

And yet the Canadian Rockies, from a strictly geological viewpoint, are not the giants of the Canadian mountain system. Technically, they are one of the smaller mountain ranges, the easternmost, and only about 100 miles wide. West of them lie the Purcells, the Selkirks, the Monashees, the Cassiars, the Skeenas, the Coast Mountains and the Island Mountains. To the layman, however, this 700-mile-wide belt of mountains is all considered to be the Canadian Rockies, so to separate them in men's minds remains somewhat difficult.

It can be said that the Canadian Rockies hold most of the memorable landscapes, the biggest mountain in Canada, the largest glacier, and most of the principal tourist attractions, particularly Jasper and Banff National Parks. They include Lake Louise, a sapphire blue lake set under Mounts Lefroy and Victoria.

But perhaps the most impressive feature of the Canadian Rockies is not a mountain at all, but a glacier: the mighty Columbia icefield which, in its thick and massive progress, moves down the side of Mount Athabasca. It reaches an abrupt climax at the edge of its own terminal moraine. Lewis R. Freeman, who traveled in the Canadian Rockies in the 1920s, saw the Columbia icefield as an immense octopus, the creeping, down-crawling glaciers springing from the main ice mass as tentacles. The mass of ice, as he saw it, rose to a high point of about 9,000 feet. "Here," wrote Freeman, "at a point not clearly defined to the eye probably of very small area, occurs the remarkable three-way split of the continental drainage. Where the tip inclines westerly, the water runs by the Bush to the Columbia and thence to the Pacific. The meltage from the northerly slope may run to either of the main branches of the Athabasca, and so on to the Great Slave Lake and down to the McKenzie and the Arctic. The east and south slopes to separate branches of the Saskatchewan which ultimately mingle with the brine of the Atlantic in Hudson's Bay."

Today, the Columbia icefield is a tourist attraction. But even as recently as fifty years ago, it was visited only after much planning and hard traveling. Byron Harmon, a photographer, spent twenty years systematically photographing the peaks of the Canadian Rockies and the Selkirks before he could consider a journey to the icefield.

Vertical rock faces challenge climbers everywhere in the Canadian Rockies. Pinnacle Peak, at 10,062 feet, is cast in the characteristic mountain form of this area—a series of sculpted eighty-degree inclined steps rising to a blunt, massive summit. If these mountains do not have steep walls, they are set in the mitre form, like a bishop's hat, an equally distinctive mark of glacial work. Mount Assiniboine, nearly 12,000 feet high, is a massive pyramid reflected in Lake Magog, with its flanking frieze of evergreens along the shore. The wanderer in the Rockies may see more than one storm flashing and rolling around this mitred peak at any time. In the peaceful serenity of his lakeside camp, he may hear the

the distant thunder of avalanches roaring down the mountain slopes far above him.

The steepness of so many of the Canadian mountains creates hazards for those who venture into them. Falling rock has claimed many experienced climbers. One excellent mountaineer, the president of Purdue University, Dr. W. E. Stone, fell off the summit of Mount Eon in 1921 because he failed to judge the treacherous rotten rock.

Despite the fact that the Canadian Rockies are modest mountains compared with the Colorado Rockies, their highest peak has few peers. Mount Robson is only 13,000 feet high, but it is set in awesome surroundings. For years it was considered virtually unclimbable.

George Coleman, an experienced climber, made an unsuccessful attempt to scale Mount Robson in 1908, and on his way down evoked the distinctive atmosphere of so much of the Canadian Rockies. "It was the 24th of September, and the autumn coloring was growing more splendid every day, the poplars taking on every rich and delicate tint, between soft green and pure gold, while the evergreens among and behind them kept their somber greens and browns. The smaller plants, roses, berry-bushes, and mountain ash, glowed scarlet and purple, and with the fine blue and green of the Jasper lake as our trail climbed upon a rocky terrace some hundreds of feet above the river there was a marvelous display of color . . ."

The mountain itself drops nearly vertically into Berg Lake, the Canadian Rockies' counterpart of Montana's Iceberg Lake. Into this lake falls a thick flow of ice, the genesis of which is the snow collecting on one face of the axhead-shaped Mount Robson. But it is unlike most glaciers. Instead of a long sinuous fall to lower altitudes, Tumbling Glacier, as it is called, drops thousands of feet in a run of less than a mile.

From lake level, the sound of the moving glacier, the pistol-shot reports of large rocks falling down the slopes of the mountain, and lightning dancing around its peak in purplish gloom create Mount Robson's unforgettable impact.

Although the Canadian Rockies rise almost directly from the Alberta prairies, they may provide insight into how radically the western American mountains modify climate from Alaska to the southwest.

When Raymond Patterson climbed the Rockies in the early twentieth century, moving through Elk Trail Pass, he looked up into the high world of the Continental Divide. "Over the ramparts of the Divide," he observed, "the southwest wind whirled great masses of spinning summer cloud. They swept over the range—sunlit, soft-outlined and glorious—and then they hit the drier air of Alberta, shredded into torn fragments and vanished against the royal blue of the summer sky. Not one faintest wisp of cloud reached the hill on which we were standing—only the wind came on. It leapt the gulf at our feet and boarded the hill with a rush and a roar, a keen, sharp wind straight from the snows, tempering the blazing sun."

Lewis R. Freeman, who had traveled widely, especially in the Andes and the Himalayas, was once caught in a Rockies storm, and he never forgot it. "My outstanding memory," he said, "was the terrific roaring of the winds among crags and cliffs which were entirely cut off from sight by the driven snow. It seemed impossible that a sound so deep and raucous could come from the friction of air on rock. Time and again I reined my horse in fear that an avalanche was descending just ahead, only to find that I was shrinking from the threat of a bugaboo no more tangible than thin air."

The Canadian Rockies convey a profound feeling of infinity, expressed by their massive march north towards their eventual meeting with the Brooks Range in Alaska. The Rockies reconcile the grandeurs of wild minarets of rock with intimate glens of tree-shrouded ponds and tinkling streams running among meadow wildflowers. This juxtaposition of opposites is a constant delight to the eye and a sustaining stimulus to the imagination. It suggests to the mountain watcher that despite the heights reached by great mountains, despite the tumult of electrical storms and hurricane-force winds at the summits, there is always a haven for humanity in the valleys.

55. Mute remnant of an ancient icefield that did not wear it down, a chimney-shaped "watchtower" rises golden in the setting sun at Yoho National Park, British Columbia.
56. Splendid peaks, reflecting lakes and ponds, characterize the Canadian Rockies. Four of the Ten Peaks are mirrored in a pond at Larch Valley, Banff National Park. Towering Mount Fay, 10,622 feet high, at left, spills glaciers down its steep sides. (J.A. Kraulis)

58. Autumn in the Canadian
Rockies flaunts brilliant yellows
as the needles of the alpine Lyall's
larch in a grove at Mount Saint
Piran at Banff National Park
change color before falling to
the ground.
59 *left*. A small waterfall
cascades over layered rock in the
Canadian Rockies. Such falls wax
and wane throughout the year,
flooding noisily in midsummer.
(J.A. Kraulis)
59 *right*. Rivers in the Canadian
Rockies rush in white tumult
toward lower altitudes. Here the
Athabasca thunders through a
deep canyon on its way to the
Athabasca Falls in Jasper
National Park.
(Edward Degginger)

60. The summit of Mount Robson (its top here hidden behind a peak in the foreground) is at 12,972 feet the highest mountain in the Canadian Rockies. Emperor Falls, fed by the great Robson glacier, drops into the Valley of a Thousand Falls.

61. Sunshine on a stormy summer afternoon highlights the braided pattern of the Alexander River meandering down a valley in Banff National Park.

62. Lightning storms like this one over Mount Hurd in the Ottertail Range of British Columbia's Yoho National Park dance across the peaks of the Canadian Rockies throughout hot summer nights. *(J.A. Kraulis)*

Hawaii's Volcanoes

The volcanoes of the Hawaiian Islands rise in great sweeps of
green, white, and gray from the benign seas around them. When they are
climbed, they reveal characteristics not harmonious with the warmth of
their oceanic home. It is often freezing cold at their summits. Snow falls
sometimes, even though balmy winds caress the shores of the islands
from which they spring. Fire and smoke rise through the snow, and
hurricane-force winds rip away pieces of pumice and lava.
The Hawaiian mountains are the visible parts of a line of volcanoes
which slowly rose from the ocean floor by spilling out immeasurable
quantities of lava from great depths, until they eventually surfaced.
All the islands in the archipelago are volcanic, but not all were formed
at the same time. Along the 1,600-mile length of the archipelago
the age of the volcanic remains ranges from 16 million years to relative
youngsters of 700,000 years. The oldest volcanoes are so well eroded and
worn down that today they have been overwhelmed by the sea, and they
only appear above the ocean at the western end of the archipelago
because coral has grown around their extinct rims and thrust itself
above the water. Every shoal, atoll, and islet along the chain marks the
place of a volcano, risen and eroded down to sea level again.
So, the highest mountains are the youngest, and they are all concentrated
at the eastern end of the Hawaiian archipelago. There the mountains
comprise the three largest islands—Hawaii, Maui, and Kauai. And only
one of these islands—Hawaii, the largest—still has active volcanoes.
Hawaii itself rises sheer from Pacific water that is 18,000 feet deep all
around it, so that the island is nothing more than a gigantic volcanic cone
towering nearly four miles from the ocean floor. The first eruption of
lava at that depth had to force itself from the sea bottom where the
pressure of the water is about four tons to the square inch, and where
the cold is intense. Those first eruptions were thus invisible explosions,
an earth force colliding with the inertia of enveloping sea.
Of all the American mountains, the Hawaiian group is easiest to
understand. They can all be climbed easily. They lie in benign
surroundings. And they are all individual, with separate personalities.
The island of Hawaii contains the two largest, Mauna Loa, at 13,677 feet,
and Mauna Kea, at 13,796 feet. These two mountains are, in their total
mass, the largest active volcanoes on earth. Mauna Loa is built up of ten
thousand cubic miles of material. It is one hundred times larger than
Mount Fuji. The island of Maui contains Red Hill, which rises 10,025
feet; Hanakauhia, 8,907 feet; Puu Kukui, 5,788 feet, and the immense
Haleakala Crater at 4,000 feet. Oahu Island has only Mount Kaala
at 4,025 feet, and Kauai Island has Mount Waialeale at 5,170 feet,
Mount Kawaikina at 5,243 feet, and Puu-ka-pele at 3,662 feet.
The process of mountain building that brought them from the floor of
the Pacific can be seen today. Kilauea, on the southeastern shore of

Kauai

Oahu

Maui

Hawaii

Hawaii, consists of a great lake of roiling red lava contained in a four-square-mile crater on top of the mountain. This lava lake within the crater, Halemaumau, has been the genesis of large quantities of molten lava. During the eruptions of 1967 and 1968, the lava poured over the rim of the crater and rolled down toward the sea. When the lava hit the water, it exploded in hissing collision. In its wake, it left a lava bed that built up the sides of the mountain another few feet.

When Mauna Loa erupted in 1926, it sent a great thick stream of lava flowing down one of its sides. It was only a relatively small eruption but it was a hint of the contained energy lying within many of the volcanoes. Mark Twain, the curious traveler, had already visited Vesuvius before he went to the Hawaiian Islands, and in comparison with the pyrotechnical displays he saw in the crater of Kilauea, he dismissed Vesuvius as "a modest pit about a thousand feet deep."

Vesuvius merely steamed and bubbled; Kilauea was a cavity of molten fire where great stark, steaming islands of cooling lava rose from boiling mud and fiery lava streams. Twain reported that: ". . . a mile square of it was ringed and streaked and striped with a thousand branching streams of liquid and gorgeously brilliant fire! It looked like a colossal railroad map of the state of Massachusetts done in chain lightning on a midnight sky. Imagine it—imagine a coal-black sky shivered in a tangled network of angry fire!"

As with most visitors to these volcanic mountains, Twain could only half grasp the vastness of what he saw. He was like the visitor who first views St. Peter's in Rome. There is nothing with which to compare the spectacle. Twain looked down into the "vacant stomach" of Haleakala and was dumbfounded by its size. "If it had a level bottom, it would make a fine site for a city like London," he noted.

Actually, much of Haleakala is as barren as any desert but is made distinctively beautiful by its sweeping, sculptured forms. Dozens of subsidiary craters lie within the main crater, and much of the interior is tinted a soft red from the iron oxides in the lava. The inside of Haleakala has none of the turbulent, jagged action of Kilauea. It has been softened, its outlines blurred and smoothed by the work of thunderous rains cutting down the walls of the crater and gradually spilling long sweeping slides of broken matter down into its center. Its true size is seven miles long, two miles wide, and half a mile deep.

All the Hawaiian mountains testify to the power of rain which shapes their soft substances. Kauai is the oldest of the islands in the chain and there the rains have sculpted unearthly landscapes. Their persistence provides an in-motion picture of how the islands at the western end of the archipelago have been broken down to sea level.

On Kauai, the rains have made more than architectural forms with their erosive influence; they have also provided the moisture necessary for plants to get a hold on practically vertical slopes. The result is a kind of artistic chaos of planed forms swathed in low green vegetation and intersected by streaming torrents of water.

Kauai's Mount Waialeale is long since extinct. Rain at its summit measures between thirty and forty feet a year. The runoff from Mount Waialeale has created such luxuriant vegetation on Kauai that it is known as "the garden island." Inside the mountain's crater a flush of fiercely competing growth makes a jungle of plants where the forces of volcanism and rain are set side by side.

The thickets of plants, the heavy mists and rains, the dripping vegetation, all make it difficult to comprehend that this is the largest of the Hawaiian craters. It is about twelve miles in diameter, but it is not the size of this crater that seizes the imagination; it is the beauty created by erosion. The ancient rains have cut down every slope and shaped triangular ridges which look as though they had been sculpted, then covered with thick green vegetation. On the northwestern side of the island, the chiseled land masses of the Na Pali coast drop steeply down to narrow beaches fronting ultramarine seawaters.

On Maui, geologists can measure the force and speed of the erosion. There, the two volcanoes are older than those on Hawaii, and the build-up of the land through eruption stopped about ten thousand years ago. The rains and winds have not much altered the outward appearance of Puu Kukui in that time. But inside, there has been impressive destruction. The fragile rim of the crater, once 7,000 feet high, is now worn down to less than 6,000 feet.

Haleakala, the eastern volcano, provides even more graphic proof of the power of the rains. They have torn down about 3,000 feet of the rim of the volcano, flushed millions of tons of debris into the crater, and gouged out canyons inside it.

The two great volcanic outlets on Hawaii Island are Mauna Loa and Kilauea, and both have made scientific study easier than anywhere else. They are close to human habitation; the climate is kind, and the Hawaiian Volcano Observatory is only a few miles from both of them. There, the genesis of explosion, of eruption, and the phenomenon of lava flow are all being studied intensively.

It has been discovered that immeasurably vast quantities of molten rock —called magma in its subterranean form—gathers power when it is still thirty to fifty miles beneath the crater from which it will ultimately burst. This mass of magma, once activated, forces itself twenty or thirty miles upward until it reaches reservoir points, or holding basins, only two or three miles from the crater summit. The force of this expanding, moving material creates great pressures within the volcano. The entire mass of the mountain swells, and the crown of the summit may rise five feet. As the magma comes pouring toward the surface, it can be measured by geologists on seismographs, traced as a series of tremors. These steady, sinister beats report that the magma is thundering through many tunnels on its way to the surface.

The interaction of volcano, soft land masses, great rains, and a kindly climate combine to create landscapes of unique beauty. The mountain watcher sees a towering pinnacle of yellow fire shooting up 2,000 feet from the crater of Kilauea. His eye follows gorgeous scarlet honey eaters flitting among the blossoms in the lush Kipahula Valley on Maui Island. He can travel from the Alakai Swamp, 4,000 feet high in the mountainous country of Kauai, to somber lava cliffs at Na Pali.

The rains in Hawaii are unlike tropical downpours. Although the monsoons of Asia may drop great amounts of water in shorter times, the Hawaiian rains fall pretty much equally throughout the year. They are carried by the trade winds blowing across the wide expanse of ocean between North America and the archipelago. This moisture would never have fallen, except as scattered showers, on the open sea. But once the moisture-laden air starts climbing the Hawaiian mountains, the moisture condenses into rain, and these rains fall tumultuously between 4,000 and 7,000 feet. At this altitude, the moisture is exhausted, and the tops of the higher mountains are quite dry.

But they continue to smoke and simmer and await the moment when they will again explode in flame and rivers of lava.

67. Volcanic action formed the islands of Hawaii and heavy rains over millions of years sculptured the lava into a mass of graceful spires in the Kalalau Valley on Kauai.

68. Early morning mist rises among the steep upper ridges of the Waihoi Valley, a rugged wilderness near the east coast of Maui. This valley, only three and a half square miles in size, reaching a depth of almost 7,000 feet, was carved from the lower flank of the great Haleakala Crater.
(Robert Wenkam)

70. A line of cinder cones crosses a rift in Haleakala Crater, its volcanic desolation now carpeted with green. The vents in the cones once ejected massive flows of fiery lava that covered the floor of the crater. *(Robert Wenkam)*

71. Waterfalls in steps drop down near the Alakai Swamp, a depression on the slope of an ancient volcano on the island of Kauai. More than fifty feet of rain a year makes this one of the wettest places on earth, with vegetation so plentiful that Kauai is known as the "garden island." *(Dan Budnick/Woodfin Camp & Associates)*

72. A cinder cone and a jagged lava pinnacle that once filled a crack in the wall lie near the rim of Maui's Haleakala Crater. Reddish tints on the cone are caused by iron oxides in the lava. 73. Haleakala, called "the house of sun," is a great shallow bowl seven miles long, two miles wide and half a mile deep on Maui Island. In the foreground are silverswords, an extremely rare plant which grows only at altitudes of between 7,000 and 10,000 feet inside the crater. *(David Muench)* 74. Streams of molten lava radiate from the Halemaumau Fire Pit, a 3,200-foot-wide depression in the sunken top of Kilauea, Hawaii's youngest and most active volcano. *(Dick Rowan)*

76. Moss, lichens, and ferns cover
a patch of lava long since cooled
on the slopes of Mauna Loa. These
early plant invaders begin the
disintegration of the lava,
creating soil for later forests.
The world's most massive volcano,
Mauna Loa, in Hawaii Volcanoes
National Park, is almost 14,000
feet and has a volume of 10,000
cubic miles.
77. A cascade of fiery lava, its
surface already cooling to form a
black crust, spills down a slope
at Kaena Point in Hawaii
Volcanoes National Park. Such
flows may move steadily at
twelve miles an hour until they
pour into the sea. *(David Muench)*

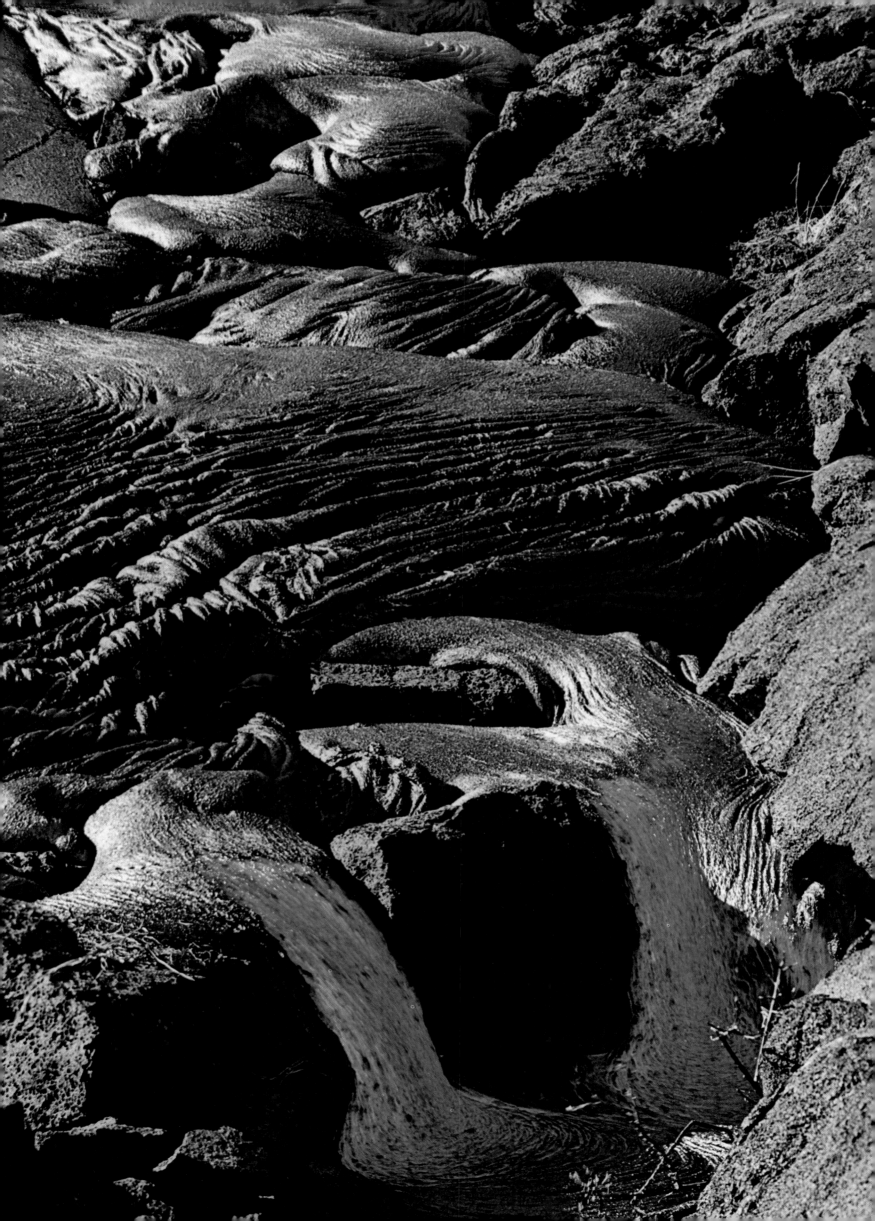

The Olympics

A fearsome god lives in the depths of the Olympic Mountains in
northwest Washington, a spirit so powerful that the flashing of its eyes
sends lightning from peak to peak, and the flapping of its great wings
makes thunder rumble among the mountains. The Indians were fearful
of this god and only ventured into the mountains when they were sure
of good hunting among the large herds of elk that roamed the river valleys.
The white men who came to the Olympics had no such fears, and they set
out to explore this jumble of rugged peaks, glaciers, valleys, and
snowfields with blithe confidence that the Olympics were just another
range of mountains and could be mastered by the simple qualities of
fortitude, daring, and climbing skill. They were wrong. There may not
be a Thunderbird god living in this magnificent range of mountains, but
there is a repellent combination of chaotic geology, vast forests,
impenetrable valleys, and confusing topography.

The forests surrounding the Olympics caught the imaginations of white
men from the moment they first saw them. They are exceptional by any
measurement. Even the staid U. S. Coast Survey, not given to hyperbole,
reported in 1858 that the Olympic Peninsula forests were an
"immeasurable sea of gigantic timber coming down to the very shores."
When Betty MacDonald, author of *The Egg and I*, saw them, she called
them "the most rugged, most westerly, greatest, deepest, largest,
wildest, gamiest, richest, most fertile, loneliest, and most desolate"
country in the world.

The centerpiece of the Olympic Range is Mount Olympus, an august and
massive mountain nearly 8,000 feet high and the origin of eight valley
glaciers radiating away from its peak. Despite its sixty-five-mile distance
from Seattle, it stands visible on the horizon on clear days like a silent
white pyramid. And the range in which it stands does not much resemble
the nearby Cascades, one hundred miles to the east. The range is
compressed into a relatively tiny area, fifty miles by thirty-five miles.
The Olympics are chaotic remnants of a once-gigantic collision between
two movements of the earth's crust. The crust buckled in the collision,
one part sinking, the other thrust up thousands of feet. Then it was
worn down, covered by the sea, and raised again during the next 60 million
years. The Olympics are sedimentary, the sandstone and shale
compounded of layers of mud and sand piled up in ancient times.

The inaccessibility of the interior Olympics has always inspired myths.
It was supposed to be the home of a legendary tribe of Indians, especially
strong and warlike. Somewhere in there was a Utopian valley, if only a
white man could find it. In 1889, soon after the state of Washington was
formed, the governor told the Seattle *Press*, "Washington has her great
unknown land, like the interior of Africa." He was certain it had
never been visited by either white man or Indian. Somehow, he knew it
was 2,500 square miles of paradise.

78

The newspaper was impressed. "Here is an opportunity for someone to acquire fame by unveiling the mystery which wraps the land encircled by the snow-capped Olympic range," reported the *Press*. James Hellbal Christie, who was to lead the *Press*-sponsored expedition into the mountains, was a Scotsman who claimed to be "a man tried by all the vicissitudes of mountain, forest, and plain." This expedition, a fiasco, did not accomplish very much except to prove how frequently it was possible for men to get lost and nearly starve to death within a few miles of civilization.

In 1890, Lieutenant Joseph P. O'Neil of the U. S. Army led an expedition which by its careful planning should have shown up Christie as an amateur. O'Neil would cross the Olympics. He would perhaps climb Olympus as well. He would take scientists with him, find trails, discover new species of flowers, collect mineral specimens, and prove that men could tame the Olympics if they only used intelligence and planning. The expedition did not have much better luck. Men got lost frequently. Trails proved delusive. The botanist deserted the party. A mineralogist and a naturalist decided to climb Olympus and put a copper box from a local alpine club at its peak. But even this was a disaster. One man got lost, and came out alone, starved. The men did climb the south side of Olympus, but did not reach the top. Even the copper box was lost,so nobody knows whether the men were even close to the summit.

Despite their magnificence of form, the Olympics are not high. Olympus' 8,000 feet dwarfs most of the other mountains. In height,therefore, they are related to the distant Brooks Range of Alaska. And like the Brooks, they rise suddenly, here literally from sea level. When Captain John Meares sailed into the strait of Juan de Fuca on July 4, 1788, and saw the mountains springing through the sea mist, dark green forest below, brilliant white snow above, he thought they were mountains fit for gods. On his chart, he marked them down as the Olympic mountains.

During the last great ice age, which ended only about 10,000 years ago, thick glaciers buried all of the Olympics except the tips of the highest mountains. They gouged out the strait of Juan de Fuca, ripped a deep trench to make Puget Sound, and cut out all the many ravines and canyons within the mountain system. Travel anywhere in the Olympics is made difficult by great wind-blown depths of snow and, for climbers, by rotted rock. Rock slides are a hazard on all Olympic slopes, particularly during the changes of season.

The myth of the verdant interior valley eventually turned out to be at least partly true. The Enchanted Valley lies thirteen miles upstream from the moist rain forests of the Quinault River, a hidden enclave walled in by steep mountains, deep in the southwest corner of the range. The floor of the valley, combining meadows and woods nearly 2,000 feet above the sea, is dotted with black cottonwood trees and wildflowers such as bright red Sitka columbine bobbing at the ends of their long fragile stems. In bloom, the flowers display the variegated colors of Nootka rose, scarlet paintbrush, purple harebell, yellow violets and the small deerfoot vanillaleaf.

Washington's first governor might have dreamed of fertile Olympian farmlands, but the geology would have confounded his expectations. Along one side of the valley a cloud-wreathed sheer cliff spouts many waterfalls, some bouncing off the rocks in cascades, others plunging straight down the side of the cliff to join the Quinault River in the valley below. It is all very spectacular. But it is no place for farmers, with black bear and elk roaming the valley, with the wooded slopes holding snow-filled chutes formed by past avalanches which may thunder into the valley during the height of summer. Olympic country is unstable, treacherous, and men must move uneasily through it.

The echo of falling rock is a distinctive sound throughout the high country of the Olympics, but almost equally characteristic are the great forests of conifers that swarm around the snow-capped peaks. These are not the highest, or the thickest, or the oldest trees. But they are perhaps the most uniformly grand forests anywhere. Because of the great amounts of rain brought in by the prevailing Pacific winds, the forests are given optimum conditions for growth. The four valleys which get most of the heavy rains face almost due west. The water-drenched winds funnel directly up them to create heavy rain forests in the temperate zone, thick carpets of ferns, great moss-encrusted Sitka spruces and big-leaf maples. The Douglas firs and western red cedars, so common elsewhere in the Northwest, are squeezed out of this world because dense forest growth stops the sunlight they need to get started. This is also the home of the Roosevelt elk, of which about 14,000 range through the valleys and lowlands—magnificent black-maned creatures almost as big as moose.

Christie's disastrous expedition showed that it was easy for men to underestimate the difficulties of moving around in these mountains. He spent more than three months attempting to find his way to the head-waters of one river. It took him more than fourteen weeks of climbing, from December to May, to discover a path through the mountains.

In fact, as it slowly dawned on men, there is no single range in the Olympics. Instead, there is a confusion of ridges and hills and valleys. The summit of Mount Olympus is surrounded by a jumble of peaks all around. Even the summit is not a single defined peak, but consists of a sprawling mass of boulders, declivities, deceptive rises, and snowfields. When L. W. Nelson, the leader of a mountaineering group, neared the summit on August 12, 1907, he thought he had conquered the mountain. But the following day he looked across half a mile of snow and saw a number of large rocks in the distance. These looked like the true summit and he led his party forward. As usual, mist swathed the peak. But when the mist suddenly lifted, he saw even higher peaks about a quarter of a mile away. Half an hour later, he and his party became the first human beings to stand on the highest part of Mount Olympus.

Later climbing expeditions got a clearer view of the summit and the surrounding territory. The Blue Glacier begins close to the top of Olympus and expands to fill the landscape around the peak.

The glacier is only three miles long, about one mile wide, more than 900 feet thick, and is moving downhill at five inches a day. If this seems odd in comparison with the longer and bigger glaciers of the north, it is fairly typical of the Olympics' other glaciers. They only cover about twenty-five square miles and there are fewer than seventy of them. The Cascades, by comparison, contain more than 600 glaciers.

The optimism of the Seattle *Press* that the Olympics contained a great asset for the state proved to be true, although not quite in the terms then envisaged. The Governor's view, in 1889, that the interior of Washington, like that of Africa, was a true *terra incognita* remains understandable today, even though the Olympics are pierced by back-packer trails and attract thousands of hikers each summer. But the torturous topography, the 100-foot-thick drifts of snow, the rotten rock, and the dense forests all combine to help preserve this compact mountain range as a difficult world to know.

81. Six glaciers descend from the slopes of the Olympic Range's Mount Olympus, 7,966 feet high, one of the tallest mountains in the Pacific Northwest corner of the United States. It was named in 1788 by an English navigator who thought it lofty and grand enough to be the home of the gods.

82. The summits of Mount Olympus are part of the snowy, rugged profile of the Olympic Range. There, thirty-five peaks rise to 7,000 feet or more, along with hundreds of other mountains that thrust upward from the deep valleys of the Olympic Peninsula. The peak of Mount Rainier, tallest mountain in the Cascade Range, bulks grandly more than 100 miles to the southeast.

84. A blue fog fills the steep-walled canyons of the Elwha Valley in April twilight. The valley, east of Mount Olympus, lies in the 896,599-acre Olympic National Park. *(Harald Sund)*

86 *left.* The rain forests of the Olympic Range abound in luxuriant plant growth. Here, a dense bank of deer fern is mixed with western swordfern. *(Steven C. Wilson)*

86 *below.* A ground-cover plant, oxalis, engulfs the buttress of a large tree in Washington's Olympic National Park. *(Keith Gunnar/ Bruce Coleman, Inc.)*

87. A moss-coated big-leaf maple hangs over the Sol Duc River in Olympic National Park. The rain forests of the Olympic Peninsula display plants ranging from creeping mosses to trees 300 feet high and a thousand years old. *(Steven C. Wilson)*

88. Rising in a majestic wall from the edge of the sea, the Olympic Range intercepts moisture-laden Pacific winds. More than 200 inches of precipitation fall on the mountains annually, most of it as snow. Coastal Indians avoided the interior, believing that the outer wall guarded a lush paradise-like valley, home of the terrifying Thunderbird, whose outstretched wings could obscure the sky. *(Harald Sund)*

The Cascades

The foothills around Mount Rainier in the Cascades contain forests of
fir, spruce and cedar growing so tall and thick in places that a highway
cut through them is a narrow canyon running through living green matter.
Some roads climb more than 5,000 feet and are cut out of rock, so that
the motorist can pass easily through country that is difficult, if not
impossible, for climbers to traverse. Here, the dramatic character of the
Cascades is easily seen. Trees sprout from nearly vertical slopes. Green
meadows, patched with blossoms, appear in mist-laden hollows. Wildflowers swarm in a suffusion of purples, mauves, whites, blues, reds, and
yellows. As one of these highways rises toward Chinook Pass, a
sense of the sharp rise and fall of these mountains grows stronger. The
road turns, and a valley appears below, apparently a few hundred feet
deep. But then, what appear to be a scattering of branches on the valley
floor reveal themselves as full-grown fallen trees thousands of feet below.
Although the peaks here are much lower than 14,410-foot Mount Rainier,
they give a persistent sense of size. They *rush* upward, many in peculiar
shapes, some like the spires of cathedrals, with the trees and vegetation
dropping away from their sides as they find it impossible any longer to
cling to the steep rock.
Finally, at 5,500 feet, the mountain slopes disappear into thick mist; but
an emerald-green tarn is embedded like a jewel in the surrounding
vegetation, which is of an even brighter shade of green. Great trees
stand like tall sentinels near the tarn.
The Cascades are "all things for all men," as one naturalist wrote of the
area. They are a climber's paradise, a museum of geological oddities which
also harbor large, and often visible, populations of wild animals. The
scenery is spectacular almost everywhere.
The Cascades are one hundred miles east of the Olympics, but unlike
those coastal mountains, many of these were built up as volcanoes, rising
from fire and sulphur and steam and molten lava. The Cascades are like
jagged teeth rising from a mass of smaller hills and mountains. The range
runs from the Sierra Nevada foothills in California to the Fraser River in
British Columbia, a distance of about 700 miles.
It is a young range. Some of the volcanic peaks are only about one million
years old. In the geological measurement of time, this is not long. These
peaks display not only the volcanic rocks of their creation, but also
sedimentary rocks from the ocean floor, some of which rose with the
newborn mountains as the lava pushed through them. All around the
mountain climber in the Cascades are signs of that ancient ocean. Shells
uplifted thousands of feet since their entrapment in oceanic mud are
fossilized in mountain rocks.
The youth of the Cascades can be seen in the steep-flowing glaciers—
nearly 600 of them—and in the dramatic Columbia River Gorge where,
before the construction of the Bonneville Dam in the 1930s, the river

dropped sharply in a maelstrom of churning water. Early explorers
named the range after these rapids. In its penetration of the Cascades,
the Columbia River comes down from the northeastern side, and then
cuts through the mountains to reach the sea.

At the northern end of the range, Glacier Peak and Mount Baker, with
its eighty-foot annual snowfall, rise among a confusion of lesser peaks.
South of them, Mount St. Helens soars in solitary grace from the woods
below. Mount Rainier, near Seattle, is the real giant of the Cascades,
although Mount Shasta, in northern California, comes close at 14,162 feet.
In the south, Diamond Peak, Broken Top, and Three Sisters rise from
plateaus that are already 5,000 feet high. The southern Cascades show
the marks of intense volcanic activity. Desolate lava wildernesses lie
side by side with beautiful grass meadows. The vents of ancient volcanoes
still tunnel through the ground, but with the lava and the steam gone,
streams now use them to travel miles underground until they burst into
view as springs. These springs create lakes where the water is caught in
ancient glacial bowls—lakes which may have no visible rivers running
into them, and no visible outlets.

In all its vistas, youth is the theme of the Cascades, and one of its
exemplars is Mount Lassen, in northern California. Lassen is the last
volcano to erupt in the United States. It blew out debris nearly four
hundred times between 1914 and 1917. But Mount Lassen is only one of
the eighteen volcanoes in the Cascades, and almost any of them could
blow up at any time. Because the volcanoes dominate all the other
mountains in the range, and because so many of them stand near
populated regions, an explosion could have catastrophic results.

These volcanoes are dormant, not dead, making it necessary to examine
the perils of eruption. Contrary to popular conception, volcanic eruption
does not take only one form—the massive expulsion of lava and debris.
A straightforward eruption might cause a sky-piercing explosion of
pumice, accompanied by a deadly cloud of gas blown miles high, and
followed by a flood of molten basalt or obsidian.

The steepness of the Cascades' slopes creates many hazards. An earthquake, or perhaps vibrations from inside a volcano when molten magma is
rushing upward, can trigger a mud slide. When this is mixed with rain
and snow, it can create an avalanche of terrifying size. Seattle is only
fifty-five miles from Mount Rainier, one of the more unstable mountains
in the range.

According to some geologists, an eruption of Mount Rainier could quite
easily destroy both Seattle *and* Tacoma. Mount Hood, another giant in
the range, could devastate Portland. The many dams that block valleys
all along the Cascades could rupture.

The ancient glaciers of the Cascades left a legacy of beauty behind them.
They carved many large hollows in the volcanic rocks, and today these

bowls contain water. Almost every vista within the mountain range provides a view of at least one lake. In some landscapes, there are several of them. The water spectacle is concentrated in the Enchantment Lakes Basin in the center of the Washington state division of the range. They are so well concealed, and so inaccessible, that they have only recently become known even to the cognoscenti among spectacle seekers and mountain lovers in America. The chain of the Enchantment Lakes, a serene harmony of rock and tree, sky and water, makes a perfect artistic statement. Fittingly, the lakes have been given names that suggest legendary qualities—Lake Viviane, named for the Arthurian Lady of the Lake legend, Grail Tarn, Valhalla Cirque, Troll Sink, and Lake Leprechaun.

The lakes are high enough to receive snow even during the summer, but this does little to discourage plant growth wherever there is enough shelter from the almost constant wind. Behind Lake Viviane is Prusik Peak, a thousand-foot chunk of rock which has dropped part of its mass to form the natural dam that holds the crystal-clear lake in place. The Enchantment Lakes are decorated by the soft delicacy of Lyall's larches, deciduous conifers which touch the region with golden yellows in the fall. These bright colors, set against the starkness of pale tumbled granite masses, suggest the ruins of an Arthurian castle. The king's sword, Excalibur, strikes out across Lake Viviane, a long line of rock extending into the water.

But the youth and beauty of the range caused only pain and suffering to man. The rugged Cascades stood in the way of pioneers, an often lethal barrier to their dreams of freedom in the west. From 1839, the pioneers crossed the Cascades in large numbers for fifty years. All along the Oregon Trail they left behind them more than thirty thousand dead, a melange of dead oxen, broken equipment, and abandoned furniture. The trail entered the Cascades near Walla Walla, Washington, and followed the Walla Walla River until it reached the Columbia River. This was the logical, level route to the coast, and it would have been the easiest, except for one fact. A scant sixty miles from the fertile Willamette Valley on the other side of the Cascades, the trail ended in vertical cliffs—the Dalles Canyon—through which the Columbia dashed onward and away.

There, the pioneers had two choices. They could abandon their wagons and take to the mountains, driving stock and lugging their belongings with them. Or they could ride the river. The rapids through the Dalles Canyon were dangerous, and many wagons, animals, men, women, and children ended their migration in the roiling waters. In 1845, a Kentucky farmer, Sam Barlow, cut a rough track through a 5,000-foot pass between Mount Hood and Mount Wilson, set up a toll gate, and charged the migrants five dollars a wagon and ten cents a head for animals.

There is a trail running the full length of the range, but no person has ever walked it in one year. Rising, falling, weaving, it takes twelve hundred miles to reach from British Columbia to California. The trail frequently runs above seven thousand feet, and is fiendishly steep in places. It often remains blocked by heavy snows until late summer and therefore does not offer the mountain walker that compressed vision of the Cascades that might make them comprehensible to one man.

When John Muir climbed Mount Rainier more than eighty years ago, he noted that the summit of Rainier was positioned between two adjacent craters, which were "like two plates on a table with their rims touching." From these craters came fumes and steam. "The unwasted condition of these craters," he observed, "and, indeed, to a great extent of the entire mountain, would tend to show that Rainier is still a comparatively young mountain."

Young and energetic, Rainier exemplifies the rest of the Cascades. Twenty glaciers radiate from its summit. It trembles with the contained fires inside it. Its sulphurous fumes drift off across ice and snow. And its summit, in Muir's words, reveals "vast maplike views, comprehending hundreds of miles of the Cascade Range. . . ." He saw interminable, black forests, and white volcanic cones stretching into Oregon. He saw the wide plains of eastern Washington. Then clouds gathered. "Soon of all the land only the summits of the mountains, St. Helens, Adams, and Hood, were left in sight, forming islands in the sky."

93. A thick summer haze veils two peaks of Mount Index in the rugged Central Cascades of Washington state. The rest of the 5,500-foot mountain is lost in a hauntingly Oriental atmosphere of mist. (Steve Marts)
94. Vaulting peaks in layered ridges separate deep valleys in the Northern Cascades, near the Glacier Park Wilderness Area. The Cascade Mountains are here seen on a hazy October morning, one of their many moods.
96. A pale crescent moon sets over Little Tahoma, 11,117 feet high, a satellite peak of Mount Rainier. Alpine firs, the commonest timberline trees in the range, cling to its slopes. (Harald Sund)

98. At 5,500 feet, alpine firs on the slopes of Mount Rainier support a heavy mantle of snow. Harsh winter storms drop up to eighty feet of snow in a year.

99. The roof of an ice cave on Mount Rainier filters out all but the blue rays of bright sunlight. *(Harald Sund)*

100. The pale light of the dawn touches the glacier-laden south face of Mount Rainier, set against Lake Louise. Originally called Tahoma, "the mountain that is god," Mount Rainier rises 14,408 feet high. *(Edward Degginger)*

102. The imposing snowcap of 10,750-foot Mount Baker, in the North Cascades, looms up in a brilliant fall landscape. *(Bob Gunning)*

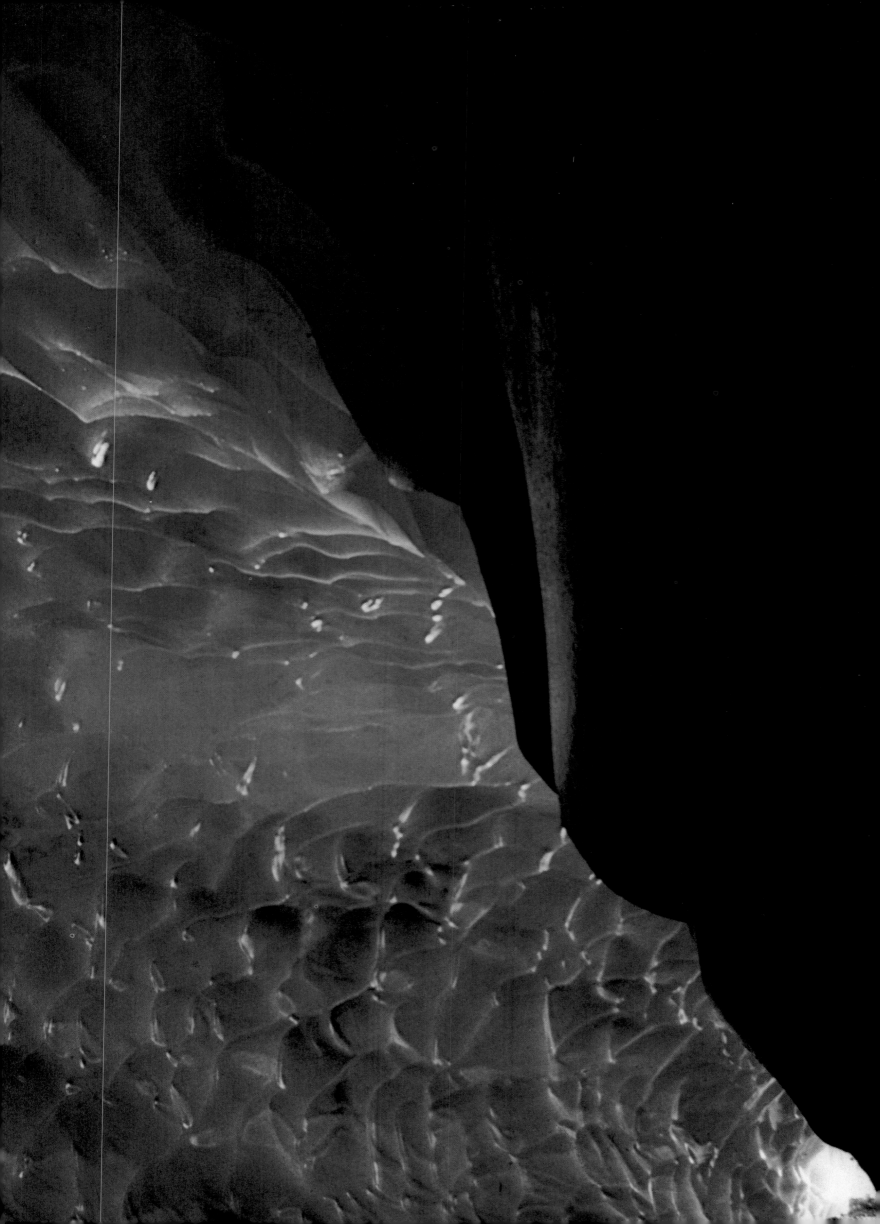

104. The noise of water falling over rocks is a characteristic sound of the Cascades. Here a stream tumbles down the Hood River Canyon in Hood National Forest, Oregon. *(David Muench)*
105. The gracefully shaped spires of firs cross an alpine meadow at Paradise, Mount Rainier National Park. The high meadows of the Cascades may not lose their snow until late July; then the wildflowers spring up in a sudden rush of growth. *(Bob Gunning)*
106. Austere Prusik Peak stands watch over Lake Viviane in the Enchantment Lakes Basin of the Cascades. This granite mountain, part of the Stuart Range, is 8,000 feet high. *(Harald Sund)*

108. The Enchantment Lakes section of the Cascades is set in a rugged region where granite cliffs impede the advance of mixed stands of whitebark pine and Lyall's larches.

109 *above*. Lake Viviane, named for the Lady of the Lake in the King Arthur legend, is a small tarn dug by glacial scouring. McClellan Peak rises to the left and Little Annapurna in the upper right.

109 *below*. Lyall's larches flank the shores of the Enchantment Lakes. They change from green to brilliant gold early in October. Then this unique fir sheds its needles like leaves, the branches remaining bare until new growth appears in spring.

110. The Lost World Plateau turns black with highlights of gold in early evening light. At 8,000 feet, the plateau is part of the Upper Enchantment Lakes Basin. Glacier Peak rises against the northwestern sky. *(Harald Sund)*

The Sierra Nevada

In March, 1872, an earthquake shook the Sierra Nevada mountains. John Muir, the Scottish-American conservationist, was in the mountains at the time. He watched as millions of tons of boulders were unleashed by the earthquake in a roar that he likened to the sound of all the thunder of all the storms he had ever heard. The deafening flow of boulders gave off sparks that were "an arc of glowing, passionate fire, roaring along a front nearly half a mile wide." Some observers of the earthquake thought the trail of sparks came from lava released by the mountains, but they were really caused by iron-hard rocks striking others of their kind.

The earthquake presented men with a dramatic picture of how, over the millennia, the massive boulders of the Sierra Nevada have been smashed into thousands of square miles of chaotically mixed rocks. Yet, despite this confusion of geologic evolution, the Sierra Nevada range—the High Sierra of literature and tradition—is compressed into one solid and comprehensible entity. The range lies along California's border with Nevada. It begins a couple of hundred miles north of Sacramento and ends, more or less, at Mojave, about 600 miles away.

Contained within this relatively narrow range, which is little more than fifty miles wide at any point, are the Donner Pass, Lake Tahoe, Mammoth Lakes, dozens of peaks topping 14,000 feet, the great Sequoia National Park, and Mount Whitney.

It also includes Yosemite Valley, some sublime wildflower upland meadows, as well as stark scenes of bare, black rock cut through by dramatic glaciers. It is decorated in many places with sequoias, the largest trees in the world. It has been called the most dramatic wilderness in America. And perhaps it is. More than five hundred peaks higher than twelve thousand feet rise along its length.

The Sierra Nevada range is nowhere near as massive, or expansive, as the Rockies, but its size still demands superlatives. One writer called it a conspiracy of climate, geology, and history which had created a "theater of stupendous size." The entire range originally consisted of a more or less solid block of rock about four hundred miles long and up to eighty miles wide, which was raised from its pivot point running along California's great Central Valley. This inclined plane of rock, broken down, tilted, and folded into itself, rises steadily to an altitude of about 9,000 feet in the northern part of the range, to about 13,000 feet in the central range, and to a peak of nearly 14,500 feet at Mount Whitney in the south.

As the range rises to the east, it comes to a great apex, which is certainly one of the more spectacular mountain sights. An escarpment up to two miles high runs like a wall along the eastern side of the range. Even to geologists, the escarpment is stunning.

The Sierra Nevada—named "una gran sierra nevada," or great snow-covered range, by a Franciscan missionary in 1776—is the central section

of three great mountain ranges that trisect the western United States.
The Coast Ranges rise nearly two hundred miles west of the Sierra,
while the Rocky Mountains lie to the east, and are separated from the
Sierra Nevada by the 1,000-mile-wide Great Basin Desert. The Coast
Ranges contain the Central Valley, low-lying and dry, but made to bloom
by man's entrapment of Sierra Nevada snow and rain water.
For John Muir, explorer and naturalist, the Sierra Nevada was the most
beautiful place on earth. His rhapsodic writings about the Sierra hid the
steel of his resolution that these mountains should be preserved, and that
people should come to recognize and love their matchless beauty.
This was quite an ambition for the age in which he lived. Even as he
wandered the rocky uplands, he could see the incalculable damage being
done to the Sierra country by hordes of nineteenth-century miners,
dam builders, lumbermen, and sportsmen. With the discovery of gold and
other minerals in the late 1850s, men poured into the Sierra and in a
few short years actually changed the appearance of the range in many
areas. One hundred thousand men came to the mountains after gold was
discovered. When silver was found, the rush increased.
Each mile of railroad track blazed through the mountains took 2,500
ties. More than forty miles of snow-sheds were built to protect trains
passing through steep valleys from avalanches. These consumed 65
million board feet of lumber, to say nothing of the even greater quantities of wood needed for bridge trestles. The silver mines took about one
billion feet of lumber for tunnel shoring. Loggers built wooden chutes, like
Roman viaducts, along which logs rode downhill at speeds of up to one
hundred miles an hour before smashing into holding ponds at the foot
of the mountains.
By the time Muir got into the alpine heights of the Sierra, most of the
Tahoe-Truckee watershed had been ruined. All that remained of the once
great forest was thousands of eroded acres of debris, scraggly second
growth, dried-up streams, and empty lake basins. Muir was possessed by
his dream to preserve the wilderness in these mountains, and founded the
Sierra Club in 1892.
Despite the destruction, despite the press of about 30 million people
living close to the mountains, the rugged terrain of the Sierra Nevada
has saved them from really serious long-range damage. The full length of
the range is such a tumble of rocks that much of it is virtually inaccessible.
Indians have dubbed the mountains "Rock Placed on Rock."
It is precisely this toughness, and the sheer durability of wilderness areas,
that gave birth to the American conservation movement. In 1864, Congress
ceded the Yosemite Valley to the state of California as a park in what
was one of the first concessions by government to the notion of
preserving the wilderness. John Muir's determination to save the Sierra
Nevada was influential in creating other national parks and forest services.

Although wilderness is the motif of the Sierra Nevada, it is no homogenized place, as are many other wild regions. Contrasts abound. The pumice-littered peak of Mammoth Mountain is stark and desolate. Nothing grows there. Yet luxuriant vegetation and soaring landforms make Yosemite a living, thriving valley. The contrasts are sometimes contained within single views. In places along the Merced River, granite walls 5,000 feet high stand next to gorgeous meadows flanking the river. The meadowlands are only a little more than five miles long, but their lofty ponderosa pines and the fragrance of incense cedar combine to make this sheltered place one of the most beautiful valleys in the world.

The Yosemite is spectacular. Ancient glaciers cut the valley down to its present U-shaped profile. Sparkling waterfalls pour down its great rock walls. One of these cataracts has a free fall of 2,565 feet. Among the valley's rocky barriers rise El Capitan, Glacier Point, Sentinel Rock, and Half Dome, themselves survivors of the glaciers.

The Sierra Nevada was born about two hundred million years ago when upthrusting rocks pushed through the silt and volcanic fallout that lay along the bottom of a Paleozoic sea. The rocks ground together with such force that the silt was compacted, and solidified into a huge mass. The silt appears today as metamorphic rock, usually a reddish or bluish color, and is the compressed residue of that early volcanic detritus. Molten granite followed the grinding rocks, squeezing between them. New volcanic eruptions buried entire mountains in debris.

This world of rock has endured because much of it would not submit to the work of the ice that came later to wear it down. The rock of the Sierra Nevada is so hard, the granite so tough, that the great ice ages appear only to have polished them. In places, the extinct glaciers rubbed the granite so thoroughly that it reflects the sun in blinding explosions of radiant light.

The Yosemite Valley holds a varied collection of granite cut and ground into an infinity of forms and shapes. These great domes are the remains of the molten granite forced to the surface millions of years ago, and contrast sharply with the valley's vertical cliffs and slender rock spires. But none of the formations appears to relate to any other. The granite domes, for example, periodically crack and lose their outer layers, which fall off in curved slabs ten to one hundred feet thick.

The mountains stand squarely in the path of prevailing winds from the Pacific Ocean. Rain storms, blizzards, and clouds are common along the western side of the range, giving the stately sequoias their home. In some places, snowfalls of more than seventy feet are possible. Yet despite the occasional savagery of the storms, and the torrents of icy rain, the high Sierra country is surprisingly benign. The temperature at the summit of Mount Whitney seldom goes below twenty-six degrees, and the air at that altitude is so dry that climbers, comfortably dressed in summer sweatshirts, can do camp chores in mid-winter.

Whitney, in fact, is rarely even white at its summit because the strong winds soon blow away the powdery snow that falls there. It shares with Mount McKinley, the pre-eminent American mountain in Alaska, the distinction of rising abruptly from low country.

The plants of the Sierra Nevada have been isolated long enough to create a distinct and unique world. The boreal forests of the Sierra are not the same as those of the Rocky Mountains, or the boreal forests of the north. There are no spruce trees in the Sierra. Instead, there are the only groves of giant sequoias anywhere, sugar pines, incense cedars, and red firs along the western side of the range, and Jeffrey pines on the eastern side.

The grandeur and beauty of the Sierra Nevada is best expressed, perhaps, by one tree. Only the western slopes of the range hold the sequoias, the largest living things on earth. About 13,000 of them survive today in a scattering of stands. The tallest of them are 300 feet high, with trunks forty feet in diameter, and some may be more than 3,500 years old. These giants are beyond any comparison.

John Muir, climbing among junipers twisted into long streamers by the vicious westerlies, witnessing the avalanches and cloudbursts, the mule deer and the bighorn sheep, the wolves and coyotes, the elk and the golden eagles of the mountains, would have agreed. There is nothing like the Sierra Nevada, and its unique trees.

115. The massive castellated ramparts of America's second tallest mountain, Whitney, at 14,494 feet, flushes deep orange in a Sierra sunrise.

116. The awesome East Wall of the Sierra, fifty-five miles long, rises more than 14,000 feet from the floor of the Owens Valley. The Alabama Hills, the weathered rocks in the foreground, were named after a Confederate ship during the Civil War. *(David Muench)*

118. Wanda Lake glistens in the twilight near the summit of Muir Pass, nearly 12,000 feet high. The clear and radiant atmosphere of the Sierra led naturalist John Muir to call these mountains the "Range of Light." *(J.A. Kraulis)*

120. The relatively benign mountain climate of the Sierra Nevada gives a surprisingly varied opportunity for plants to grow. A cluster of Alpine Sierra primrose finds a small niche in a granite wall near Elizabeth Pass.
121 *above*. Barren, sloping, granite cliffs, so vast they dwarf the few pines on a lower ledge, are typical of the Elizabeth Pass area in the western Sierra.
121 *below*. Spring ice rims Precipice Lake in a high pass in the Sierra. *(Sonja Bullaty and Angelo Lomeo)*

122. A centuries-old Sierra juniper, shaped by the wind, thrusts out of tumbled rock at Carson Pass in the eastern Sierra. Winds there often blow steadily at over sixty miles an hour. *(David Muench)*

124. Great columns more than 200 feet high, white firs and ponderosa pines are shrouded in fog in Sequoia National Park on the western side of the Sierra Nevada Range.
125. After a late spring snowfall, icicle streamers form on boulders in Sequoia National Park.
126. The dark red trunks of the world's biggest trees, sequoias, rise behind snowcapped boulders in Sequoia National Park. *(Sonja Bullaty and Angelo Lomeo)*
128. A spring dawn touches Stoneman Meadow, Yosemite Valley, with the great mass of Half Dome obscured at the right in a luminous early morning fog. *(Harald Sund)*

130. The peeling surfaces of
Quarter Domes at Yosemite Valley
reveal how the layers of their
granite core have fallen away
over millions of years.
(Galen A. Rowell)
131 *above.* With a serenity
characteristic of the region, the
Merced River is touched by a May
dawn in the Yosemite Valley.
The bulk of El Capitan looms on
the left and the spires of
Cathedral Rocks on the right,
with Bridalveil Falls barely visible
in the dim morning light.
131 *below.* Yosemite Valley during
a lightning storm, with El
Capitan, Cathedral Rocks and
Bridalveil Falls seen from left
to right, forms a dramatic
spectacle. *(Harald Sund)*

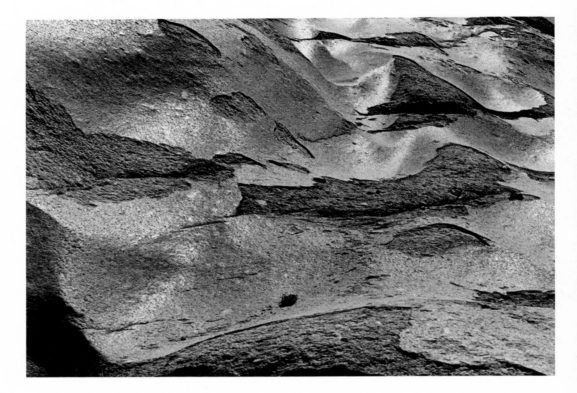

132. The sheen of highly polished
rocks shows the work of long-gone
glaciers which scraped over the
granite in Tuolumne Meadows
above Yosemite. *(David Muench)*
133. Rich emerald-green moss
smothering boulders in the
Tuolumne River Canyon in
Yosemite National Park is typical
of luxuriant vegetation stimulated
by ample rains. *(Steve Crouch)*
134. A meadow of purple lupines
surrounds a live oak in the grassy
western Sierra foothills. Soon
after the March rains, such
luxuriant scenes disappear.
(Sonja Bullaty and Angelo Lomeo)
136. East of the Sierra, soft
green hills are dusted with tiny
spring flowers in the Cholame
Mountains. *(Dick Rowan)*

The Rocky Mountains

The great range of the Rockies, the Continental Divide, which in effect separates the Atlantic from the Pacific, is difficult to describe as an entity because the human mind must see things only in relationship to dimensions that can be measured, understood, and compared with something else. One writer has described it as an ocean of rock in a storm. It consists of thousands of very large mountains. On a day when the clouds lie low at the middle altitudes, an observer may stand on the Great Divide and see twenty-two peaks towering up out of the white fluffy clouds and stretching out of sight.

Within this system, inside the North American continent alone, there are sixty mountain ranges. The great Brooks Range of Alaska is the northern beginning of the range; the New Mexican desert is its temporary terminus within the United States. The system goes on south, through the eastern section of the Mexican Sierra Madre and so on down through South America's Andes. The total length of the Divide, with all its windings back and forth, is about 25,000 miles.

Within the United States, excluding Alaska, the Rockies consist of three parts—north, central, and south. The Northern Rockies are confined to Montana and the borderlands of Idaho; the Central Rockies are Wyoming country; and the Southern Rockies are mainly in western Colorado.

In 1609, a group of Spanish colonists, led by Don Pedro de Paralta, established a village at the base of the Sangre de Cristo Mountains and called it La Villa Real de la Santa Fe de San Francisco, the location of modern Santa Fe. For 200 years, the Spaniards held dominion over the Southern Rockies, a hold not really broken until the beginning of the nineteenth century, ending finally when Mexico separated from Spain in 1821.

Before the Spaniards were gone, the United States had made some attempt to find out what lay beyond these ramparts. In 1803, President Thomas Jefferson sent out Captains Meriwether Lewis and William Clark to explore all of the Louisiana territory and find a route to the Pacific. They went through the Northern Rockies, to the Columbia River, and reached the Pacific in 1805.

Lieutenant Zebulon Pike was the next notable American mountain explorer, sent by the United States Army a year or so later to explore the Rockies. Pike did not do so well. His entire party nearly starved in the Sangre de Cristo Mountains. Then they were captured and imprisoned by the Spanish and ended up in a jail in Chihuahua before being released in 1807.

Commerce and the pioneering spirit eventually opened up the Rockies, just as they had pushed men through the eastern Appalachian Mountains, across the prairies, and along the Texas shores and rangelands. The first persistent travelers to the Rockies were trappers. The California Trail was blazed in 1833 by a trapper born in Virginia, Joseph Reddeford

Walker. These men spearheaded the advance into the Rockies largely because of the War of 1812 with Britain. The aftermath of the war brought a big demand for beaverskin hats. The smart dressers of Paris, London, and New York demanded beaver, and, obediently, the trappers pushed west. Beavers then thrived almost throughout the Rockies' lowlands, where they had dammed up mountain streams and colonized valleys. Scots and English, Spaniards and French Canadians, moved in to kill them.

Actually, many of the trappers preceded the War of 1812. John Colter got into the Yellowstone country as early as 1808, and was perhaps the first Anglo-Saxon to see the geysers there. In 1810, Andrew Henry was in the Teton country in winter. The Great Basin of Nevada was penetrated by Joe Walker and Jedediah Smith in the 1820s at the same time that Ewing Young and his party traveled from Taos, New Mexico, into California. The Great Salt Lake was reached in 1824 by Jim Bridger, Etienne Provost, and Peter Skene Ogden.

These men, working in parties or alone, crossed back and forth over Rocky Mountain country with a thoroughness that was to give all later travelers an excellent idea of the difficulties and dangers of mountain life. In 1843, John Charles Fremont covered the Oregon Trail and most of California. The Northern Rockies were systematically explored in 1853 by Isaac Ingalls Stevens.

These trailblazers led the way for naturalists and scientists who were beginning to enter the Rockies by the late 1860s. Two of the most celebrated were John Wesley Powell and Ferdinand Hayden, who made a careful study of the natural history and geology of large parts of the Rockies. Gold was found near Denver in 1858. Miners slogged through the old South Pass through the Wyoming Rockies and the trail across the southern desert of New Mexico and Arizona after James Marshall's discovery of gold in the American River of California in 1848. The great Comstock silver lode was uncovered soon after the Denver discovery. The Rockies of Montana yielded gold. The silver boom of the 1870s in Colorado's mountains helped create towns like Leadville and Aspen.

All during this time, the Rockies were explored by true mountain men. They were a distinct and unique breed. The trappers became legend with their capacity to cover long distances in pursuit of their prey, to endure great hardships in their lone journeys through the wildest country. When men became fugitives, they were often pursued by the trappers and prospectors who had made the mountains their own. The men of the Rockies and the other western mountains laid bare their mystery and turned them into magnets to draw the rest of America westward. In this way, the Rockies in particular put a special imprint on the American mountain experience and all of American history thereafter.

Northern Rockies

The theme of the Northern Rockies is one of spaciousness, interrupted repeatedly by signs of destruction and rehabilitation. Ice was here very recently. The great ridged mountains are so demonstrably cut by the action of sheets of ice that they look like a child's sand castle shaped by a blow of his shovel. But within miles of such stark scenery are rich carpets of meadow flowers blooming near the snows. There are lichen-covered rocks decorating the steep slopes of the mountains.

These mountains, like the rest of the Rockies chain, began their major uplift about 70 million years ago when mountains were growing all over the world during the Laramide Revolution. This rising of the land went on for more than 30 million years. It pushed the rocks, many with a mantle of sediment from ancient seas, up above the ocean. But these northern mountains have only very recently finished the work of their formation. The Rockies in the north are not especially lofty, but they are extensive, spread across range after range—the Bitterroot Range, the Salish Mountains, the Lewis Range, the Big Belt Mountains, the Beaverhead Mountains—which encompass, at their northern end along the Canadian border, Glacier National Park.

Frequently, the mountains and the sky unite to form a single primeval scene. Clouds gather thickly, dark on the undersides, gloomy caps over dusky rock, the brilliant cobalt sky surmounting all. From their ridged lines across the sky, the clouds throw black shadows across the mountains. They turn valleys into stygian gashes across the gray, brown, and white landscape. On every side, the turbulent rock ocean of peaks tumbles away into the distance.

Here, the mountains are not as massive or as high as in central Colorado. But these mountains are different in appearance. Instead of bulk, there is elegance. The minareted pinnacles of rock sparkle with dustings of snow and ice.

A visual oddity which can be seen from the tops of the highest peaks is the difference between the western and eastern sides of the mountains. As with all the continental western mountains, the western side is humid and the eastern side is dry. But in Montana, the contrast is extremely sharp. On the west, before the slopes of rock pinnacles begin, the vegetation is almost as lush as along the Pacific northwest coast. The soil smells rich; moss flourishes everywhere; groves of giant red cedars stand silently except for the sough of wind in their high foliage.

But then, scarcely ten miles away, on the other side of the Divide, the land becomes as desolate as the moon. The rocks still show the abrasion of glaciers in the bright morning sun. The mountain goats pick their way across steep rock walls, snipping off tiny shoots of vegetation. By the time the Pacific air reaches the east side of the Rockies, it has already exhausted most of its moisture.

Many travelers in these Northern Rockies, most particularly in the spectacular Glacier National Park which encompasses a dense cluster of peaks and glaciers set against the Canadian border, have compared the colors with those of the Grand Canyon. If there is a comparison, it is one that is upside down geologically. The Grand Canyon has been cut by the Colorado River to reveal ancient strata. In Glacier National Park, the strata have been thrust up so high they appear near the summits of the mountains.

The work of glaciers here was thorough. One of the largest cirques in the Rockies' system contains Iceberg Lake, near the Canadian border, an immense bowl about a mile in diameter. This spectacular bowl is enclosed by nearly vertical sides. One of its banks rises steeply up Mount Wilber to its peak at 9,000 feet. The snow and ice slides down the walls of the lake, piles up along its shores, and then drifts out as miniature icebergs.

The Northern Rockies parade their warm and colorful aspects in many ways. In August, even though the summits are snowcapped, the glaciers are moving, and chunks of ice fall into Iceberg Lake, the slopes of the hills change color with the appearance of flowers.

But the upper altitudes of the northern United States Rockies are pure Arctic. There the mountains compress the essence of Arctic and temperate zones into one intense series of images that gives them their power and their charm for the mountain watcher.

141. Grandeur characterizes the Northern Rockies, as seen here where the Salmon River winds through a V-shaped valley cut into the mountain rocks of central Idaho. *(Maurice Hornocker)*

144. Rising Wolf Mountain towers in the background of Young Man Lake in southeastern Glacier National Park, Montana. Reputedly so inaccessible that only a young man could reach it, the lake nestles under the curved ridge of Flinsch Peak. *(Dan Budnick/Woodfin Camp & Associates)*

142 *above*. Mount Oberlin and Mount Gould loom in the background at Glacier National Park. Flowers flourish in the Hanging Gardens of Logan Pass. *(David Muench)*
142 *below*. In the highest parts of the Northern Rockies, a massive jumble of peaks and the white slashes of glaciers combine to make Glacier National Park chill and austere. *(Dan Budnick/Woodfin Camp & Associates)*
143. Bright patches of lichens create intricate patterns on the slopes of Mount Reynolds at 9,000 feet in Glacier National Park, Montana. *(David Muench)*

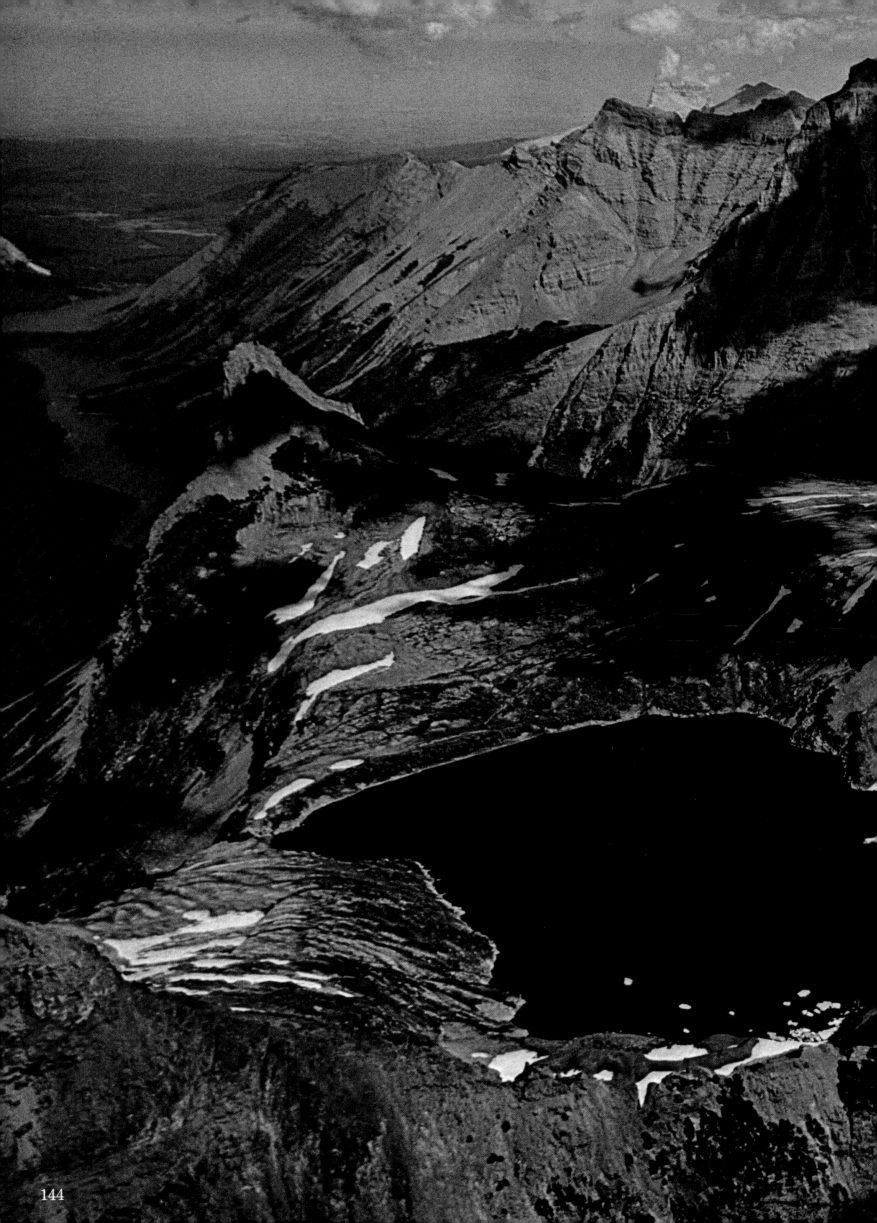

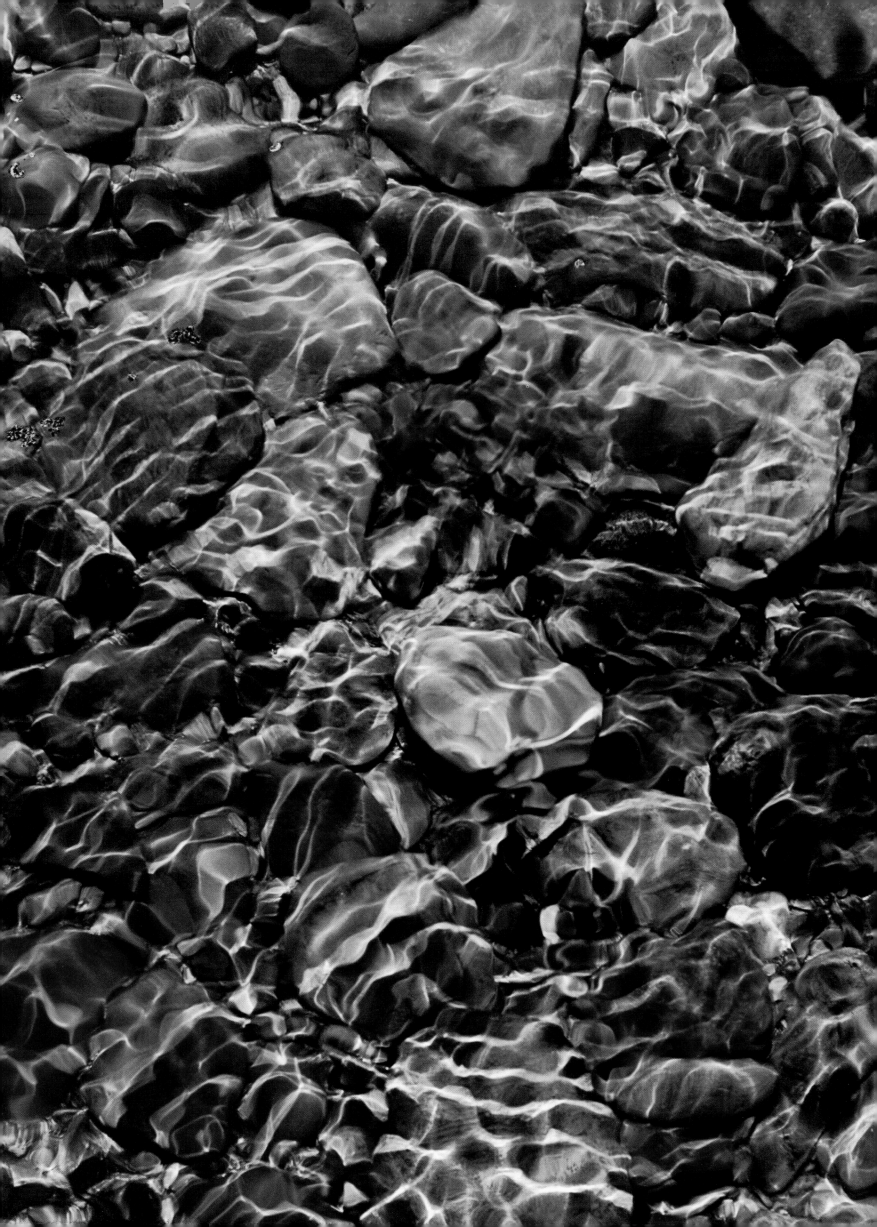

146. A miniature mosaic of geological history is displayed in the stones under shallow water at McDonald Creek in Glacier National Park, Montana. *(David Muench)*
147. In early fall the peaceful Belly River winds serenely along the base of Bear Mountain in the northern part of Glacier National Park near the Canadian border. *(Dan Budnick/Woodfin Camp & Associates)*

Central Rockies

The Grand Tetons are a shock to the eye, not because of sheer height, but because they climb so steeply from the flatland before them. These great chunks of rock, some absolutely naked, others thinly touched with grass and trees, have a structural, cathedral-like eminence, closely akin to something designed by a man with a sublime imagination.

Almost every one of the peaks of the Teton complex, which runs along the western side of the upland plain containing the Wyoming town of Jackson, has its own character. On one, the vegetation struggles upward for thousands of feet, while on a neighboring peak, everything has been swept away in a series of rock slides and avalanches, the side of the mountain consigned to a pile of rubble in the valley below.

One writer, Fritiof Fryxell, attempting to describe this stark raw landscape, first mentioned the cathedral image, and it is a good one. He noted that it could be expanded by the sight of ". . . the profiles of countless firs and spruces congregated like worshippers on the lower slopes; it reappears higher in the converging lines of spire rising beyond spire; it attains supreme expression in the figures of the peaks themselves that, towering above all else, with pointed summits directs one's vision and thoughts yet higher."

The Tetons, forty miles long and ten miles wide, have been described as the "most splendid" of the central Rocky Mountains, but they are only a tiny part of the central Rocky Mountain system, which includes the Crawford Mountains, the Wyoming Range, the Gros Ventre Mountains, and the Snake River Range. The Tetons are not a part of the Continental Divide. It passes through the high plateau of Yellowstone, east of the Tetons, and south through the Wind River Range, with its 13,000-foot peaks, its many small glaciers and extraordinary canyons. Tireless Mark Twain saw something of the Central Rockies in his passage through South Pass, one of the breaks in the Great Divide which lies at the end of the Wind River Range: ". . . we sat . . . contemplating the first splendor of the rising sun as it swept down the long array of mountain peaks, flushing and gilding crag after crag and summit after summit, as if the invisible Creator reviewed his gray veterans and they saluted with a smile. . . ."

Twain was not even high in the mountains at that particular point, yet his view of the Rockies overwhelmed him. The pass is only about 7,550 feet above sea level but Twain thought he could see forever. "These sultans of the fastnesses were turbaned with tumbling volumes of cloud, which shredded away from time to time and drifted off fringed and torn, trailing their continents of shadow after them; and catching presently on an intercepting peak, wrapped it about and brooded there—then shredded away again and left the purple peak, as they had left the purple domes, downy and white with new-laid snow."

With the discovery of gold in the Southern Rockies in 1858 near Denver, a flood of prospectors spread throughout the mountains. The nineteenth century search yielded gold, silver, copper, lead, zinc, molybdenum and other minerals. The experiences of the prospectors illuminated the character and nature of the Rockies. They lurched through deep drifts, died in blizzards, went blind with the brilliant light flashing off the snow. The ice has left its distinctive imprint everywhere. In places, particularly along Wyoming's Wind River Range, the mountains are pot-holed with cirques. Sometimes, two cirques come together so that the barrier between them is nothing but a ragged-edged ridge on which the persistent frost action is constantly chipping away bits of rock.

From the air, the cirques appear as countless dark jewels set in the midst of masses of white-dusted soaring rock. There is a symmetry and beauty about them that suggests a deliberate force at work spotting the lakes or tarns precisely at the places where they will best decorate the bleak landscape of rock and snow. When these lakes are set very close together, separated only by a sharp ridge of rock, the western tarn drains into the Pacific, the eastern to the Gulf of Mexico.

Many Rockies climbers have complained that when heading toward a peak, they were constantly fooled into thinking that the ridge ahead of them was the last. Invariably, they found another ridge, then another, and another. One explorer noted in his diary that he would reach the foot of a mountain in one day. It took him six days. By such measurements, the size of the Central Rockies grows in the mind.

149. A glacial basin hewn from rock by a long vanished mass of ice now becomes a pretty interplay of tree and water and rock in the Green River lakes at the foot of Square Top Mountain in the Wind River Range of Wyoming.

150. In some places ancient ice sheets left little except bare rock, the starkness here enhanced by a storm retreating from Island Lake in the Bridger Wilderness of the Wind River Range in Wyoming. *(David Muench)*

152. The Snowy Range of Wyoming is decorated with scattered marble fragments, here seen under the mass of Medicine Bow Peak. *(David Muench)*
153. At 7,000 feet, a flower-bordered stream smokes with mist in Yellowstone National Park in the spring. *(John Deeks)*

154. The Yellowstone River, in
its swift course through
Wyoming, has cut a valley out of
volcanic rock to a depth of a
thousand feet. *(Claude Haycraft)*
155. A grayish-toned terrace of
travertine, formed by waters
depositing calcite over long
periods, is spread out under a
stormy sky in Yellowstone
National Park. *(Harald Sund)*
156. The rich evening coloration
of the Teton Range dominates the
background in this impressive
view of the Central Rockies from
Jackson Lake in Wyoming.
(David Muench)

Southern Rockies

Major John Wesley Powell brought an almost psychic understanding to the meaning of mountains and to the Southern Rockies in particular. He thoroughly explored all the territory south to the Grand Canyon. His classic "Report on the Lands of the Arid Region," published by the Federal Government in 1878, was a detailed and brilliant description of the geography, resources, and value of the mountains to Americans generally. He measured the mountain country in terms of the livestock that could be grazed, the timber that could be harvested or preserved, the amount of water that was available, and what should be done to develop it.

The Southern Rockies are a broad, deep complex of mountains with many great peaks, and they are the most dramatic representation of the force that created the Rocky Mountain system, the Laramide Revolution of about 70 million years ago. But Powell was less interested in grandeur and the fact that his group of mountains contained 1,200 peaks higher than 10,000 feet and fifty-three higher than 14,000 feet than he was in conserving a priceless resource. He foresaw that the mountains, despite their massiveness and scope, were vulnerable to man's works. They could be destroyed by overgrazing and by the savage exploitation of their timber. His report and his work triggered some of the earliest preservation legislation, particularly the Forest Reserve Act, in which President Benjamin Harrison signed thirteen million acres into permanent Federal Reserve in 1891. This insured the vital flow of water from the mountains and so helped sustain the expanding civilization around the mountain ranges. Even greater conservation works by President Theodore Roosevelt followed: he set aside more than 200 million acres of forest and mineral areas for preservation, much of it in the great mountains.

The Southern Rockies are found mainly within the borders of Colorado. This is mineral country and, in distinct contrast to the Central Rockies, men have occupied, exploited, and colonized these mountains more thoroughly than any other part of the system. The mountains come together here in a sea of rugged peaks, wide as well as long.

Here is the Front Range, the Park Range, the Sawatch Range, where the original foundations of the Rockies have been uplifted into the jagged pinnacles seen today. Here is the Mosquito Range, consisting of sedimentary rock not yet worn away by erosion. Here, too, the Sangre de Cristo Mountains, where the Spanish first entered and occupied the Rockies, and the San Juan Mountains. Here is the Rio Grande Valley, and the immense line of 14,000-foot peaks marching down the Sawatch Range: Mount Elbert, Mount Harvard, Mount Columbia, Mount Yale, Mount Princeton. It is, perhaps, small wonder that soon after this explosion of upthrusts the Rockies diminish, change character and so begin a transformation that leads to the New Mexican desert.

But not before the San Juan mountains have had their moment. They are huge, covering more than 10,000 square miles. In fact, they are the largest range of mountains inside the United States section of the Rockies. And, as befits a place of transformation, the San Juans are a mixture of landscapes and of geological forms. They include granite spires that would be at home in the central section of the Colorado complex. They sprawl in masses of eroded material streaming down from rounded summits, their slopes colored russet and red by oxidizing iron.

And in the San Juans are suggestions of the desert to come. Dwarf cedars and yuccas line some of the valley streams and Engelmann spruce —high-altitude trees which can climb mountains of pure rock—crowd around sheltered lakes, all set against bare brown and gray peaks that look parched.

Dr. Ferdinand Vandiveer Hayden, a physician and one of the most distinguished of all American geologists, mapped all of the San Juans, much of the other Colorado Rockies, a feat he accomplished in only three years, between 1873 and 1876. He, like Powell, seemed especially responsive to and inspired by these mountains. He had a sharp and intelligent eye for almost every part of the natural historical process. Hayden's work in these mountains left a timeless imprint: five mountains are named after him, along with a town and a lake. He left behind him an indelible impression of one man's enthusiasm inspired by the phenomenon of rock upthrust from the face of the earth.

159. Aspens, seen here in the San Miguel Mountains of Colorado, flourish in the Southern Rockies, colonizing most of the lower slopes and valleys and putting on a rich display of color in autumn. *(David Muench)*

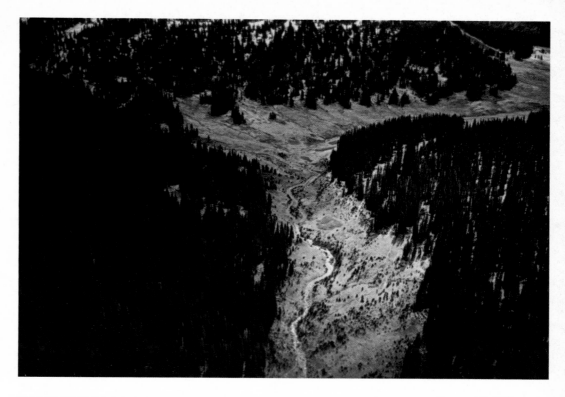

160. Deep orange alpenglow on 14,256-foot Longs Peak, with Chasm Lake in the foreground, contrasts with a morning storm building behind the peak in Rocky Mountain National Park. *(Kent and Donna Dannen)*

161 *above*. The San Juan Mountains of southern Colorado lie between the desert country to the south and the more luxuriant growth of temperate regions to the north. The sun sparkles on a winding river. *(Dan Budnick/Woodfin Camp & Associates)*

161 *below*. In Colorado, green alpine meadows reach high into the peaks of the Rockies. Here a meadow mantles the side of Mount Evans. *(David Muench)*

162. The towering mountains of the Northern Rockies here give way to a chaotic sprawl of peaks in the Front Range of the Colorado Rockies. *(David Muench)*

164. Groves of aspens, such as this one in the Rio Grande National Forest of Colorado, flourish in the Southern Rockies. *(David Sumner)*
165. Water and rock interact as the Twin Falls drop into Yankee Boy Basin in the San Juan range of Colorado. The San Juans border the desert to the south, but parts of the mountains are well watered.
166. The first storm of winter dusts the Sneffels Range with snow in the Dallas Divide in southwestern Colorado. The snow catches in the branches of yellowing aspens not yet free of their leaves. *(David Muench)*

The Desert Mountains

The mountains of the American southwest neither form long ranges
nor cluster in large masses. They are, instead, spaced across wide
expanses of desert and near-desert. If they have anything in common,
it is the quality of mystery that men have attributed to them. From the
earliest days of the white man's entry into this region, the mountains
drew prospectors. One writer claimed that the desert air bred fables,
"chiefly of lost treasure."

The mountains abound in the legends and the abandoned mines of
treasure-seekers. Gold is found in the Sonoran desert mountains; silver
came out of the Pinal Mountains near Tucson; the Silver King mine
yielded a spectacular, though short-lived, bounty of gold; the Kofa
Mountains of southwest Arizona also gave gold. The ruins of rusted
machinery, caved-in diggings, and shafts filled with squeaking bats mark
many of the mountains. Drought did not faze the early exploiters; they
dug deep wells to tap water, and they hauled wood from hundreds of
miles away to shore up their treacherous tunnels.

The southwest mountains are a patchwork of ranges that stretch from
California to Texas. They include the ranges flanking Death Valley,
the isolated Henry Mountains and the Uintas of Utah, the Big Horn and
Sacramento Mountains of Arizona, and the Superstition Mountains
miles to the east, as well as clusters of mountains in western Texas.

The surrounding deserts give these mountains a unique character. "Death
and life usually appear close together," wrote Edward Abbey, a confirmed
"desert rat" and desert mountain climber, "sometimes side by side, in
the desert. Perhaps that is the secret of the desert's fascination: all lies
naked, out in the open in this all too vulnerable land." However, it is
not merely dryness and heat that characterize these towering masses
of rock. At the conjunction of Colorado, Utah, New Mexico, and Arizona,
temperatures range from nearly 30 degrees below zero to 115 degrees
above—a span of 145 degrees. Great extremes of weather may be
experienced in a single day.

The mountains are also deceptive, for the human visitor at least,
inspiring a misleading confidence. Areas of towering limestone ledges,
spires of sandstone flanking deep canyons alternate with thick groves
of gambel oaks, and oceans of brilliant yellow flowers carpeting ground
briefly moistened by rains. The exceptional clarity of the light
contributes to a feeling of freedom and exhilaration.

Mountain and desert are both subject to the ravages of erosion. The arid
landscape, scorched by months of drought, is rarely capable of growing
a protective mat of vegetation. When rain does come, it falls in torrents,
and the erosion is awesome. Granulated rock, crumbled sandstone and
limestone and dry dusty soil sweep across flood plains, pour into canyons,
and race along in red, yellow, and brown streams.

From the air, many of these mountains look as though they have been

cut by a knife. Vertical-walled canyons seem to have sliced through soft
rock. Rain-cut slopes slump downward in rolling masses of debris. In
Death Valley, the alluvium spills from the surrounding mountains and
spreads out in wide fans. The massive destructiveness of this erosion has
broken down most of the southern desert mountains to relics of their
ancient size. Some geologists believe that the Colorado Plateau, the arid
center of the meeting of four states, has lost about 10,000 feet of surface
material to erosion since its formation.

The ruins flank or encircle most of the arid flat areas in Arizona, New
Mexico, and western Texas. The great arid expanse of cactus country that
stretches across the southern-central part of Arizona, for instance,
is surrounded on all sides by mountains—the Buckskin, New Water,
Eagle Trail, Gila Bend, Mazatzal, the Superstitions, Pinal, Santa
Catalina, Huachucah, and Santa Rita. The mountain watcher can stand
in the foothills and see Tucson on one side, the Santa Catalina mountains
on the other. From Phoenix he can see the Superstition Mountains to the
east, the Big Horn Mountains to the west, the Mazatzal Mountains to
the north. At Gila Bend, he is in the lee of the Gila Bend Mountains.

The Superstitions are typical of the desert mountains. Standing 30 miles
east of Phoenix, they rise steeply from desert floor. They are as
incongruous an addition to the landscape as the man-made ziggurats
rising from the flood plain of Mesopotamia. Jacob Waltz, a Dutchman,
created the legend of a "lost mine" in the late nineteenth century
because of his periodic disappearances into the Superstitions.

Despite the dryness, a remarkable variety, if not abundance of plant and
animal life has established itself in practically every part of this great
southwestern mountain region. Snows pour down the slopes into the
desert, where the water prompts brief but spectacular surges of plant
and animal life. Mountain pools created by brief rains or snow swarm
abruptly with microscopic forms of life as well as toads and frogs. The
squawbrush and mountain mahogany crouch low against the ground,
their small leathery leaves covered with a wax surface that prevents
excessive evaporation.

Wherever streams and rivers run, plants and animals gather along the
lifelines of water. Crickets teem along the banks of the Colorado River
where it flows through bare, red rock country. Hummingbirds hover,
wings whirring with a strange loudness in the still air. The yucca plant
raises its thin, graceful stalk hung with pendant yellow blossoms from
what appears to be absolutely dry sand. A mile away, a solitary green
juniper springs from equally dry land.

More than 140 species of cactus flourish in the Sonoran Desert. These
superbly adapted plants have also colonized all of the dry areas of most
of the southern mountains. They range from huge plants like the organ
pipe, which may take 130 years to grow 30 feet, to the tiny, crouching,

many-stemmed hedgehog cacti. All are adapted to storing vast amounts of moisture during the brief rain storms. Thus prickly pears have an extremely efficient system of roots, and exist in deserts where practically nothing else survives. But they are equally at home in the mountains and can be found more than a mile high, even in areas that do get snowfall.

Like other sections of the Continental Divide north of them, the La Sal Mountains rise gently to their snow-covered summits from the desert floor. The foothills catch the barest sprinkling of rain, which falls as snow on the mountains in the background. Although desert surrounds it, the La Sal range grows a green cover of phlox, balsam root, bladderpod, Indian paintbrush, snowberry bushes, bluegrass, and dandelions. The northern slopes of the La Sal foothills contain groves of quaking aspens sustained by sporadic rains.

The La Sals have none of the grandeur of the northern mountains. They appear as not much more than a jumble of rocks, remote and lonely on the horizon. Against the vast expanses of the desert, they appear diminished, even dwarfed, an impression that is banished only when they are approached. Then tall, stark peaks rising into pale blue skies create an impression of majestic isolation, which many observers find awesome and at the same time saddening.

Desert mountain country casts a spell over the visitor. For some, it is a sense of the supernatural; for others, desolation. For most, it is a feeling of being in the presence of the unknown. The Indians attributed something supernatural to almost every mountain. The region is full of ghosts and legends of ancestors and gods. The buttes, the mesas, the canyons, the precipices, all have been imbued with legendary life by both Indians and pioneers.

Long silences, broken only by the sound of zephyrs touching dry leaves, become presences in the imagination. The extraordinary clarity of the air tends to magnify objects in the distance, and makes them seem deceptively close.

Such an atmosphere was not lost on ancient peoples. The Indians of southern Utah invested one peak, Navajo Mountain, with deeply religious significance. According to legend the tribe was once caught in a big flood, but it escaped through a huge hollow reed. Soil from Navajo Mountain was collected, and from six other mountains, all sacred to the Navajo, in which the reed was planted so that the tribe would always have a means of escape should disaster strike again.

Navajo Mountain is a solidified lava core with a cover of sediments. Seen from a distance, it does not look particularly large or unusual. But when the climber begins ascending it, he scales a steep talus slope studded with boulders as big as houses. By the time he has reached the top of the talus slopes, he is 2,600 feet high and his view of the flat landscape around him is breathtaking.

The heat, the hot dry winds, the expanses of desert have not stopped mountaineers from exploring the southwest mountains with the same kind of enthusiasm that enabled them to conquer the northern peaks. They have climbed most of the cathedral-like spires of stone that rise from level Utah landscapes, such as the rectangular column of horizontal layers of sandstone known as Castle Rock. They have scaled gigantic El Capitan, and Agathla Peak in Monument Valley, both beautifully sculptured cores of volcanic rock which rise from miniature foothills of debris.

When mountaineers reach the summit of these desert mountains, they do not always find rocks baking in the sun. Some of the ranges are high enough to reach and catch rain which the desert around them rarely receives. The climber at the top of the Baboquivari Mountains of Arizona, a 40-mile long range sprung from utter desert 8,000 feet below, may trudge through Pacific rain. Or he may rest among flourishing plants.

If the day is clear, other mountains are visible from the summit the Santa Catalinas, the Ajos, the Huachucas, the Aque Dulces, and even the Gulf of California, 150 miles away. Dust storms whip across the desert below. In a sheltered crevice, snow glistens in the white sunlight. Such are the surprises, the contrasts, the extremes, the qualities matched nowhere else, that make the desert mountains unique.

171. Death Valley, California, is flanked by two mountain ranges, the Panamint and the Amargosa. Here the ridges of the Panamint Range, seen from Telescope Peak, march into the distance. From such ranges as these comes the eroded rock that forms the sand of the Death Valley desert.

172. The San Jacinto Mountains, which stand between Palm Springs and Los Angeles, are a startling contrast to the stark floor of a stony desert. Here Mount San Jacinto dissolves into the haze of one of the occasional desert storms.

174. Every line of these southern desert mountains, seen here from Zabriskie Point in the Golden Canyon of Death Valley National Monument, speaks of the erosion from ages of rainfall. As the mountains are worn down, their detritus creates the deserts of the Southwest.

176. As the Colorado River cuts its way south through southern Utah, it passes the eroded columns of the Fisher Towers on the left. The snowcapped La Sal Mountains rise in the background. *(David Muench)*

178. The Fremont River Canyon cuts through the Henry Mountains of southern Utah. This compact range, dominated by Mount Ellen at 11,615 feet, lies west of the impounded Colorado River at Lake Powell.

179. The Henry Mountains cover only about 400 square miles but they concentrate all the rich variety of color typical of the desert mountains.

180. The Pine Valley Mountains of southern Utah are compact, like the Henry Mountains, and share the same vivid colors, the same contrasts between desert and the snow on the mountains. *(David Muench)*

182. A limestone reef projecting above the softer material around it provides a typical west Texas scene in the Sierra Diablo. Great erosion marks the southwestern mountains as seen in this divide between two canyons.

183. The south rim of the Chisos Mountains in Big Bend National Park of western Texas overlooks the Punta de la Sierra, a volcanic range that is a part of the Rocky Mountain system. *(Jim Bones)*

184. The mass of El Capitan rises from the Guadalupe Mountains of western Texas and southern New Mexico, near the Carlsbad Caverns. The peak is part of a limestone reef that has resisted erosion. *(David Muench)*

The Appalachians

When André Michaux climbed Grandfather Mountain in North Carolina in August of 1774, he joined with his companion and guide in singing *La Marseillaise,* and then cried out: "Long live America and the French Republic! Long live Liberty!" Michaux was convinced that he had climbed the highest mountain in North America. In fact, Grandfather Mountain is lower than 7,000 feet, and in terms of the great American Mountains is not much more than a high foothill.

Nevertheless, Michaux's ascent was a notable moment in the annals of American mountaineering because it was contrary to the attitude that had prevailed among Americans since the continent was settled some two hundred years before. The Appalachian chain of mountains snakes down the eastern shores of North America from Newfoundland almost to the Gulf Coast of the United States. Although not continuous, in the sense that the Cascades, the Sierra Nevada, or the Brooks Range of Alaska are, it remained a formidable barrier to any movement west, inhibiting both colonial travel and commerce. For more than two hundred years, it was considered too much trouble and too costly to lug household belongings, farm equipment, livestock, and families over the Appalachians to reach farmland which, it was known, lay on the other side of the mountains.

When the great western mountains have been examined, this seems rather ludicrous, because the Appalachians, by comparison, are nothing more than large hills. The most impressive collection of mountains anywhere along the chain is the Presidential Range in New Hampshire, which includes a cluster of peaks—Washington, Adams, Madison, and Jefferson—of which the highest, Mount Washington, is only a little more than six thousand feet.

Yet despite their lowly size, and their lack of really formidable peaks, the Appalachians have a collective impact that is indisputably their own. None of the western ranges is so continuously a coherent whole. The Appalachians stretch about two thousand miles, beginning with the low ranges of western Newfoundland, going through the Shickshocks of Quebec, running into the New Brunswick and Maine mountains, becoming the White Mountains of Vermont. They are the Berkshires of Massachusetts, the Catskills of New York, the Appalachian Ridges of New Jersey and Pennsylvania, and the Alleghenies of southwestern New York. All of them lead to the Blue Ridge of Virginia, the irregularly shaped Cumberlands of Virginia, Kentucky, and Tennessee and the Great Smokies. One can walk the length of this chain of mountains on the Appalachian Trail. The hiker must be prepared, however, to walk more than two thousand miles to get from Mount Katahdin in Maine to the termination of the trail in northern Georgia.

The sprawling mass of the Appalachians contains many extremes, as is, best indicated by the climate at the tops of the unimposing

mountains. The heights are unimpressive—2,500 feet in the Long Range of Newfoundland, 4,000 feet in the Shickshocks of Quebec, 5,000 feet in Maine, 6,200 feet in the White Mountains, 4,400 feet in the Green Mountains, 2,100 feet in the Blue Ridge Mountains, 2,000 feet in the Pennsylvania ridges, 3,000 feet in Maryland, 6,000 feet in the Smokies—but the summit weather can be ferocious.

Blizzards sweep across Grandfather Mountain in North Carolina, while the lowlands, six thousand feet below, are cool and misty with cows grazing on green grass. Hikers and climbers, caught without suitable equipment in unseasonable storms, die on New England mountains. The weather on the top of Mount Washington can blow at more than two hundred miles an hour in gusts, and the temperature goes far below zero. While the age of the western mountains is measured in scores of millions of years, the Appalachians approach the billion-year mark. Almost anywhere in the chain a museum collection of rocks lies beneath the walker's feet. Everywhere the eye travels there are signs of this great age.

In Vermont, the hiker stumbles across gneiss more than one billion years old, or finds marble almost half that age. Even the sandstone seen in Maine with seashore fossils in it is probably more than four hundred million years old. Vermont slate and Massachusetts limestone are equally ancient.

Many of the vistas from Appalachian peaks resemble one another in their serenity. Whether they are seen in the rolling, mist-covered hills of the Great Smokies, or in the patchwork quilt of colors in an autumnal New England forest, the outlines are rounded, soft, peaceful, giving rise to the myth that the Appalachian system is uniform when, in fact, its life forms are diverse.

The trees are the rightful inheritors of Appalachian territory, since they flourished in the wake of retreating glaciers, endured destructive mankind, and are today making a triumphant comeback throughout the chain. Almost every mountain, hill, and valley is studded with trees struggling to recover their ancient right of tenure after more than two centuries of logging, burning, and slashing by settlers. The immense destruction of Appalachian forests was accomplished during the nineteenth century when three-quarters of Connecticut was denuded, more than half of Maine was cleared entirely, and five-sixths of the Great Smokies was devastated by logging. Now, with state and federal preserves established, private and public conservation efforts succeeding, and the abandonment of many marginal farms, the forests are returning. In a hundred years, or less, the forests of the Appalachians will be as they were when white men first laid eyes on the magnificent white pines of the north, and the oak and the chestnut groves of the south. The Appalachian system has survived into triumphant old age, able once again to protect its ancient hills with a thick cloak of trees.

Southern Mountains

The blue haze that hangs in the air of the Great Smokies is often so thick that the sun plays tricks with it, sometimes setting it alight with aquamarine fire, other times enriching it with sparkling, crystalline colors. Above the haze, bulky clouds add to the dramatic decoration of the mountain air. At sunset, light shafts through broken dark clouds. Then, as the sun sinks, sapphire becomes deep purple, and the wooded peaks stand out sharply defined against the golden sunset. Sometimes clouds settle into the valleys of the Great Smokies and only the tallest peaks rise above them. One of these, Clingmans Dome, at 6,652 feet, is the highest peak in eastern North America.

The atmosphere of the southern Appalachians is created by trees. The mountains, with one hundred and forty different species, have a quality of dusky, brooding quietude that suggests mystery rather than the serenity implied by the New England mountains in the chain. And yet, when the southern mountains are climbed, a link is apparent with the north. One walks among Fraser's firs, which is a southern relative of the northern balsam fir. The red spruce is the same as the spruce in the north. He may see Canada mayflowers, trilliums, and wood oxalis.

Parts of the Great Smokies are as wild as anything in New England, the Adirondacks, or in the Rockies, yet many of the southern peaks are ascended, not by well-marked hikers' trails, but by well-paved highways. In North Carolina, Grandfather Mountain and Mount Mitchell both have roads running high up their sides. And across the North Carolina and Tennessee border, Roan Mountain and Clingmans Dome can both be climbed by well-trampled paths to their summits—Clingmans Dome has an observation tower on top.

Indeed, the wilderness areas have been so well developed that the traveler's conception of the mountains is almost totally conditioned by the automobile. When he drives along the Blue Ridge Parkway going south, Grandfather Mountain's double peaks stand alone before him, beckoning him to climb them. And climb he can, to five thousand feet, on a toll road.

The press of population against these mountains—against the entire Appalachian chain, for that matter—is so great that there is not much space left for the kind of mountain contemplation provided by an old horse trail snaking up and down hill and mountain toward the south. This trail is now the Blue Ridge Parkway, which vaults to five thousand feet offering magnificent views to the east, west, and south on its way to North Carolina.

Roan Mountain provides another kind of view, mountain meadows at 6,313 feet, which are dotted with flowers and thick masses of catawba rhododendrons. These gorgeous stands of shrubs are placed as if the terrain had been landscaped by a master artist. The hiker can walk between them along avenues and paths that look man-made.

The mosaic includes two quite characteristic parts of the southern mountains—the balds and the coves. The balds are puzzling grassy patches which interrupt the thick forest cover and occur toward the peaks of many of the southern Appalachian mountains. The coves were formed when mountainside erosion carried down material and deposited it on terraced valleys near the bottom of the slope. These coves give one simple and direct benefit to struggling vegetation. The soil, so gathered, is deep and fertile. They are cut through with the streams that helped to form them, and are often riotous gardens of blossoms and flowering trees. Some are packed with sugar maples. One of them, Cades Cove in the Smokies, covers several square miles and is a parade of trees, shrubs, wildflowers, game, and fish.

The early settlers sometimes used both the coves and the balds to raise sheep. The animals spent their summers on the cool, wet balds where grass grew thickly, and then were brought down three thousand feet to winter in a cove at a lower altitude.

The mosaic pattern of the southern Appalachians is a fascinating variation on the American mountain experience. The Great Smokies, with their pastel colors and luminous mists, are in their age of retirement. They stand as a valedictory to America's young mountains, still locked in their struggle against levelling erosion.

189. The atmosphere of the Great Smokies is created by veils of mist lying in its softly rounded hollows, clinging to its ridges and thick forests, and sometimes swathing its highest peaks. Subtly changing colors mark the seasons. *(Larry West)*

190. Spring comes early at Stone Mountain, Georgia, where the delicate greens of newly opening leaves begin to obscure the pale granite cliff behind them. *(William A. Bake, Jr.)*

192. A quiet summer stream
bubbles through moss-covered
stones in the Smokies.
193. All parts of the Great
Smokies proclaim their age.
Already split by frost action,
this rock is slowly being eroded
by the coating of moss and lichens
covering it. *(Larry West)*
194. The seasons of the Smokies
move at a slower pace than in the
north. Autumn brings a leisurely
change of trees from green to
hints of yellow and brown.
(John Earl)

196. A temperate forest at the
base of Stone Mountain, Georgia,
turns orange as the full impact
of the fall spreads across the
South. *(William A. Bake, Jr.)*
197. Aging has gone on so long in
the southern mountains that trees
and shrubs have claimed the
earth for themselves. Here, the
precipitous Linville Gorge of
North Carolina is being overtaken
by autumn. *(John Earl)*
198. Winter begins on the
summits of the Smokies. At 6,000
feet the trees are rimed with ice,
the branches frozen, the hollows
thickened with dense winter mist,
while the lowlands around the
mountains are still green.
(William A. Bake, Jr.)

Hudson Highlands

The Hudson Highlands have none of the high altitudes and sweeping slopes that characterize the rest of the Appalachian Range. Instead, they are an almost self-contained region of ever changing succession, low-key scenes of old mountains slowly coming to the end of their reduction from high peaks. The Hudson Valley runs through the heart of the Highlands, and the river has cut a spectacular gorge there. It is an eye-catcher, winding past the celebrated Storm King Mountain. It flows by Breakneck Ridge, where a wild bull once roamed the woods, according to pioneer legend, then fell over the ridge and broke its neck.

The Highlands are a meeting place for northern and southern plants and animals. Tundra bog moss and subarctic black spruce thrive there in environments close to groves of southern trees. Northern birds such as blackburnian warblers and brown creepers work through the higher woodlands where some southern birds reach their northern limit.

The river narrows and quickens in the gorge as the Highlands lift more than 1,000 feet.

The Highlands were once more than 10,000 feet high, but most of their mass has eroded away in the past 600 to 700 million years. The present hills are part of the remnants of what was a mountain system comparable to the present-day Rockies. Actually, the Highlands are among the oldest masses of land anywhere in North America, thrust upward in the Precambrian period, 1.2 billion years ago, and thus are close in their time to the ancient Canadian Shield.

There is striking evidence in many places of the most recent glacial advance, during the last part of the Pleistocene: immense boulders perched isolated on meadow slopes and ridges. The boulders are of different rock from the Highlands bedrock and were undoubtedly transported by the ice from farther north.

The Highlands link the higher parts of the Appalachians north and south of them with a narrow band of ancient rock not more than twenty miles wide along their southern flanks near Peekskill, just reaching into Connecticut and the Berkshires and the Massachusetts Highlands in the northeast, and merging into the Jersey Mountains in the southwest.

The Hudson River flows past the spectacular Palisades, which runs along the western bank of the river opposite Manhattan and for some distance to the north. The Palisades are the termination point of the Newark Basin, and are not related to the Hudson Highlands but gave man easy access to its rock. This rock—red sandstone—although found in the Highlands, is only a small part of its mass. The rock was once used as the main ingredient in the construction of the brownstones of New York. From the Palisades also came a rock, called Belgian bluestone in the days it was being quarried, which provided the millions of cobblestones once used in New York City street paving, patches of which are still visible under worn layers of asphalt.

In height, the Palisades match the sides of the Highlands gorge cut by the Hudson. Their forty-mile length and the regularity of their vertical lines so impressed early voyagers that they named them after palisaded villages of local Indians. River steamers burned wood that was cut from the top of the Palisades and pitched down into the water. Wealthy New Yorkers, whose homes were heated by fireplaces, bought sections on top of the Palisades each with its convenient "pitching place."

Although the Hudson Highlands are a part of the Appalachians, they are less distinctive than the nearby Catskills, which have 4,000-foot altitudes and rose to their present height in a series of gentle lifts beginning about 350 million years ago. But the Catskills were not the first choice for the Indians or the colonists for permanent occupation. It was not until men had the need for tanning materials from the great hemlocks of the region that they began exploiting the Catskills, making them a center for the industry for many years. The felling of the hemlocks opened the land to sunlight, and other trees, such as birch, maple, oak, and other hardwoods, came into dominance.

The Hudson Highlands are thus a quiet interlude in the Appalachian chain. Lacking the raw drama of heights and widespread uplifts, they brood quietly through the seasons, a refuge for plants and wildlife along the river from Newburgh to south of Peekskill. They speak with the quietest voice, to man, of any of the American mountain areas.

201. A long series of escarpments from an ancient uplift, the Shawangunks, overlooking the Hudson Valley, thrust out rocky shoulders near New Paltz in New York State.
202. The Hudson River escarpment reaches a dramatic point in the steep Palisades of New Jersey, here clothed in a winter garment of mixed deciduous trees.
(Ralph Weiss)

204. The northernmost sections of the Catskills are folded and densely forested. They are eroding but at an almost imperceptible rate.

205. A mixed stand of ash and other deciduous trees have taken over a wet pocket in a valley at Harriman State Park in the Hudson Highlands.

206. Victim of lightning or gale-force winds, a fallen hemlock, hundreds of years old, slowly decays and returns to the soil in Harriman State Park, New York. *(Ralph Weiss)*

Adirondacks

The Adirondacks are not a geological part of the Appalachian chain. They are an extension of the Canadian Shield, and so are related to Quebec's Laurentian Mountains. But they are much grander than the Laurentians. Forty-six peaks in the 4,000-foot scale sprout from a wilderness as big as the state of Vermont. The Adirondacks are related to the Appalachians, however, in their quiet and aging dignity. When autumn haze swathes the mountains, it blurs their outlines, fills in the hollows rounded by ancient glaciers, and softens the landscape to an intimate and peaceful wilderness. The fall raiment of the trees—red spruces and balsam firs, beeches and maples, oaks and hemlocks—creates an atmosphere that is quite different from any found in the great mountains of western America. The eastern mountains have always had devotees just as partisan and idealistic as John Muir was about the Sierra Nevada. The Adirondacks' champion was Verplanck Colvin, a lawyer's son. By the time he was eighteen, in 1865, Colvin was determined to be an explorer and map-maker of the entire Adirondack area.

He was convinced that the Adirondacks were sacred as a wilderness preserve and as a watershed for the City of New York. He persuaded the state legislature to survey the mountains and to appoint him the state surveyor. He walked practically every part of the region, and his work led to the formation of the Adirondack Forest Preserve in 1885 and the establishment of the Adirondack Park in 1892. In 1872, while exploring Mount Marcy, he found that a small lake, set in the hills, flowed "not to the Ausable and St. Lawrence, but to the Hudson," and thus discovered the headwaters of the Hudson River. He named the tiny tarn Lake Tear-of-the-Clouds.

This lake is almost pure fairy-tale material. It sits alone in a surrounding mass of densely wooded slopes. Seen from the right aspect, the lake catches the color of the sky and throws it back like a small and brilliant mirror.

From any dominating point in the Adirondacks there are visible signs of age, very old age, carrying with it the special serenity that is part of all the eastern mountains from Newfoundland to Alabama. The top of Haystack Mountain in the Adirondacks offers a stunning vista of rounded summits undulating to the horizon.

The age of the Adirondacks, and of all the eastern mountains, is much greater than that of any formation in the West. The measurable history of this mountain complex began well over one billion years ago. Then, most of eastern New York was under water, and the shallow sea received much of its silt from the nearby land. The erosion was great, and the sea, which stretched from present-day Labrador down to the Gulf of Mexico, received lava, volcanic ash, sand, and clay which gradually solidified into a seven-mile-thick mass of sedimentary rock.

Then the seabed sank and the earth's mantle buckled. The mountains were thrust up perhaps twenty thousand feet. But within about 600 million years, the Adirondacks had been eroded almost flat. One hundred million years later—about 400 million years ago—mountain building began once more. All the five modern ranges of the Adirondacks were formed then, as were the major mountains of New England.

The Adirondacks cover such a wide area that they remained a virtual wilderness until very recently. Even today, although they are penetrated by millions of people each year, they remain wild, and unexplored to all but the most determined backpackers. Their survival as a wilderness, set so close to the teeming population of the eastern seaboard, is a testimony to the extraordinary farsightedness of Verplanck Colvin and to all those who followed him and perpetuated his ideals.

209. Birches climb the side of Cascade Mountain in the central high peaks of the Adirondacks, catching the last rays of late afternoon sun in January. *(William A. Gardner)*

210. The lofty beginnings of the Hudson River, Lake Tear-of-the-Clouds, near the top of the Adirondack peak, Mount Marcy, was not discovered until 1872 when Verplanck Colvin thought he saw it ". . . dripping with the moisture of the heavens." *(Robert Perron)*

212. Mount Marcy's rock-strewn summit, at 5,344 feet the highest spot in the Adirondacks, is the viewing platform for Haystack Mountain and other summits in the rugged High Peaks area. *(Dan Budnick/Woodfin Camp & Associates)*

213. The upper and lower Ausable Lakes form a dramatic scene in the main range of the Adirondacks. *(Albert Gates)*

214. An intimate closeup of the origins of the Hudson River, delicate Lake Tear-of-the-Clouds, is overhung with morning mist. *(Robert Perron)*

New England Mountains

The New England ranges in the Appalachian chain all have distinct personalities. The Maine mountains are enclosed in the forbidding atmosphere of the north. Great uniform forests sweep up to the bare, rock-broken heights of Mount Katahdin, the highest peak, and the other mountains of the region. Several hundred miles to the south, the Green Mountains running down the spine of the state of Vermont, which was named after them, are friendly landmarks for both visitors and natives. Their gentle slopes have acquired a luxuriant green cover which is lightly dusted with new snow in early winter. By contrast, the magnificent White Mountains of New Hampshire can be treacherous for such comparatively low peaks. In fall, their white birches blaze with brilliant color. White haze works its misty way through the trees, and high ponds sprout the dead trunks of drowned trees.

In all of these northeastern mountains, the process of erosion has been going on for so long that, unlike almost everywhere in the west, it is not dramatically visible. The eastern mountains have become dwarfs reduced from their lofty fifteen-to-twenty-thousand-foot peaks. Their rocks have been smashed by ice, ground down by glaciers, gullied and chiseled by tumbling water, avalanche, and landslide.

Although the New England mountains are nowhere as old as the Adirondacks in their basic substance, they were thrust up at the same time as the Adirondack peaks. This occurred about 400 million years ago when mountain-building began. In the Adirondacks, this acted on rock laid down more than a billion years ago. In the New England mountains, it worked on sedimentary rock laid down by ancient seas that once covered all of New England. The White Mountains of New Hampshire were thrust up, the Green Mountains of Vermont were squeezed into towering outlines, Mount Katahdin was pushed upward.

After that came a long period of calm and relative inactivity while the infinitely slow process of erosion again brought the mountains down. Ice sheets came down at least four times, crushing the land, dropping debris, grinding the mountains once more, gouging out the valleys. The mountains are still recovering from the great depression of the Pleistocene. Many tiny earthquakes touch the region as the land is readjusted by the internal forces of the earth.

The great age of the New England mountains and their very slow reduction by erosion provided ideal environments for climax forests of great size and of varied species. Majestic white pines flourished in groves sprinkled throughout with other forest trees.

The white pines brought the British swarming through the forests, and the best trees were always marked for the king's use, to the rage of the local people. But it was the American, not the Briton, who most threatened the white pine and all other trees in the New England mountain forests. More than half of all the trees in New England and the Adirondacks were felled in the nineteenth century.

Mount Katahdin might still be devastated by logging and fires were it not for the fact that it was bought by Percy Baxter, a wealthy Maine legislator who was then governor. Baxter began buying parts of the mountain in 1930, and continued until after World War II, when he owned it all. Then he donated the mountain to the people of Maine.

The Appalachian Trail starts at the top of the peak and leads down mountain and up hill, through valley and swamp, above and below the treeline. It is just possible for a determined and serious hiker to begin at Mount Katahdin in the alpine spring and complete his journey to Georgia by October. There he will be among the southern trees in their autumn colors. He will have walked through fourteen states, climbed 6,642 feet to the top of Clingmans Dome in the Great Smokies, and tramped twenty miles above the treeline in the White Mountains of New Hampshire.

The mountains of America are extraordinary natural history, within reach of everyone. Henry David Thoreau climbed Mount Katahdin in 1838 and wrote, "There was clearly felt the presence of a force not bound to be kind to man." All the mountains are dangerous to those who do not know them. But they are also filled with delights. One of these is the sight of the rising sun seen from the summit of Mount Katahdin, the first light to strike America each day.

217. A mingling of deciduous trees and conifers fringes the slopes of Vermont's Green Mountains in winter. (Sonja Bullaty and Angelo Lomeo)

218. The stark rock-swept peak of Mount Katahdin in Baxter State Park in Maine is the first point in the continental United States to be touched by the morning sun. (Dan Budnick/Woodfin Camp & Associates)

220. One of the giants of the
Presidential Range in New
Hampshire, Mount Washington,
here deep in winter, is reputed to
have the worst weather on earth.
(Clyde H. Smith)
221. Chimney Pond, at Mount
Katahdin in Maine, is littered
with boulders that have been pried
loose by frost. *(Dan Budnick/
Woodfin Camp & Associates)*
222. On a clear day, a view from
the chin of Mount Mansfield,
at 4,393 feet the highest point in
Vermont's Green Mountains,
reveals the White Mountains,
including stately Mount
Washington, which, at 6,288 feet,
is the highest peak in New
England. *(J.A. Kraulis)*

This book was prepared and produced by Chanticleer Press, Inc.
President: Paul Steiner
Editor-in-Chief: Milton Rugoff
Managing Editor: Gudrun Buettner
Project Editor: Susan Rayfield
Production: Helga Lose, Irene Valles
Maps: Roberta Savage
Design: Massimo Vignelli